Face-to-Face Selling

Bart Breighner

Park Avenue

Face-to-Face Selling

© 1995 Park Avenue Publications

Cover Design: *Robert Steven Pawlak*

An Imprint of JIST Works, Inc.
8902 Otis Avenue
Indianapolis, IN 46216
Phone: **1-800-648-5478**

Library of Congress Cataloging-in-Publication Data

Bart Breighner

    Face-to-Face Selling / revised edition / Bart Breighner.

           p.   cm.
      Includes index.
      ISBN 1-57112-065-3 : $9.95
      1. Selling.   I. Title
      HF5438.25.B725   1995   94-21279
      658.8'5–dc20   CIP

03 02 01 00 99   9 8 7 6 5 4

Printed in the United States of America

This publication is designed to provide accurate and authoritative information in regard to the subject matter covered. It is sold with the understanding that the publisher is not engaged in rendering legal, accounting or other professional service. If legal advice or other expert assistance is required, the services of a competent professional person should be sought. From a declaration of principles jointly adopted by a committee of the American Bar Association and a committee of publishers.

Contents

CHAPTER 5

CHAPTER 6

CHAPTER 7

CHAPTER 8

CHAPTER 9

CHAPTER 10

CHAPTER 11

CHAPTER 12

CHAPTER 13

APPENDIXES

Foreword

Not another book on selling! No—a tremendous book on selling! A book on selling that will become the basic reader you'll return to time after time for a tune-up on attitude and technique. Bart has given us a book on selling that is different: He demonstrates his selling expertise throughout the book by adding sizzle to the basics.

When Vince Lombardi used to tell his players they were going back to basics, he would hold a football in his hand and say, "This is a football." To the reader, that's an amusing anecdote about a great coach and motivator. But if your sales manager uses a similar approach—holds out a book and says "This is our basic sales manual"—it's not so amusing, especially if you think you have more advanced problems. Your reaction to the back-to-basics approach is probably "Kid stuff." or "This is not my problem!" But if you can keep the sizzle in your basics, you not only will enjoy going back to them but you'll grow to the point where you never leave them.

One of the qualities of a professional is the ability to identify and empathize. Bart does this beautifully with his face-to-face selling philosophies and techniques. The world badly needs more and better sales professionals. This book will make a tremendous contribution toward satisfying that need, and I hope to introduce it to millions.

Charles "T" Jones

—Author, *Life Is Tremendous*

Introduction

WHO NEEDS THIS BOOK?

Here's the answer to that question: everyone who ever considered or began a career in selling.

Yes, this book is about selling. But it's not just for salespeople. It's for anyone who can benefit from learning what I call "the art of creative confrontation."

You Want to Become More Persuasive

If this is your goal, you will find that by absorbing the philosophy of this book and by using the techniques discussed here, you'll become a stronger, more effective person in all your dealings with others.

You Are New to Selling or Are Considering It

If you fit into either category, this book can be your "survival kit." It will help you handle the setbacks that new salespeople face. It will give you an understanding of the law of averages. It will clarify in simple terms the creative sales process that will enable you to turn prospects into buyers—and leave them glad they bought!

You Are an Experienced Salesperson and Doing Great!

Tremendous! Then this book will help you stay on the roll you're on and give you the impetus you need to make even bigger things happen. It will show you that you are doing a lot of things right and remind you of some things you need to begin doing again. It will trigger your brain into action to cash in on new opportunities that exist for you right now!

Does This Book Apply to Your Particular Situation?

This book will definitely be an asset to any experienced salesperson, and it's an absolute must for anyone starting out in sales. Actually, this book can have a positive influence on any person, regardless of vocation. But as with any other useful tool, its benefits depend on its use.

It's a book on the *sales process*. This book will help you "get into your own head," set your thinking straight, and renew your own attitudes about selling yourself! Everyone sells himself or herself every day in one way or another. This book will show you how to feel confident in front of "prospects," demonstrate how to give a smooth, open-minded presentation, and how to tap the benefits of solid sales techniques.

Are you a "recruiter" in your line of work? This book's for you. Do you have to regularly get up in front of people and sell an idea, a concept, or a product? This book's for you. Do you need to plan a strategy to conquer shyness or fear when giving a demonstration? This book's for you.

Some reviewers have said that they would universally recommend this book just for the solid information and advice found in key chapters.

So you see, whatever you do, you can use the skills explained on the following pages. It makes no difference what type of work you do or what type of selling you are involved in. The principles discussed in this book involve dealings with people, not just products or services. It really doesn't matter whether you are selling in homes or businesses. It makes little difference whether you are demonstrating a product on a one-to-one basis or dealing with groups of people in a "party plan." Because there are so many common elements in the "people business," a high percentage of the ideas put forth in this book are certain to apply to you.

Much of what you do in your personal life is "selling" someone else on something, from influencing the choice of a restaurant or a movie to proposing marriage. A lot of daily living comes down to persuading someone else to accept the idea or proposal that you believe in.

So whether you knock on a door to sell Avon, work for one of the fine companies that use the party plan, or call up someone to see if you can get an appointment to sell an insurance policy—you'll find lots of good ideas in this book that you can use in other ways every day. And, of course, if you do choose a career in sales—well, I'm going to teach you everything I know about what it takes to succeed.

Q: What Is Face-to-Face Selling?
A: Getting Through to Someone

The expert waiters or waitresses who serve your food with a flourish and make you feel like their best customer are getting through to you. They're selling the merits of the restaurant itself. They're selling the quality of the food. They're sending you home with a full stomach and a warm, comfortable, pampered feeling that is sure to bring you back. By doing the job right, they are "pre-selling" an undetermined number of other meals that you will buy at that restaurant because you will want to come back for more.

The doctor who talks to you in a gentle, soothing manner when you are in pain or upset about some annoying symptom is getting through to you. He is selling you confidence in his professional skill. He is selling you on the importance of following his advice carefully and diligently. He is selling you on the fact that what he does is worth the bill his secretary will hand you before you leave!

The auto mechanic explaining your car's problems...the sixth grader sweet-talking you into letting him mow your lawn so he can save money for summer camp...the preacher, the plumber, and the politician—they're all trying to get through to you. They are "selling" you. And their selling skills are what determine their success or failure.

Face-to-face selling is the art of convincing, the use of learnable techniques to close a transaction, and the application of basic rules to show a prospect or customer that you have something he or she needs. It is not conning, not intimidating, and definitely not one-way communicating.

Perhaps best of all, every chapter of this book can stand on its own. Any chapter could be used alone. Every chapter is valuable in its own right, and any one of them will give you "your money's worth."

CHAPTER ONE

Selling in the
1990s

Thirty-five thousand feet up in a Boeing 747 over the Pacific—four hours into a fourteen-hour flight from San Francisco to Hong Kong. The meal has been served and the film has just come on. The flight attendants have some free time.

Karen Robinson, married and the mother of two teenagers, from a suburb of St. Paul, Minnesota, has been a flight attendant for eighteen years. She comes into the galley and says to her co-workers, "Hey, guys, I'm into a new business, and I'm really excited about the products we offer. You wanna see 'em?"

They do, so she reaches into her carry-on luggage and brings out a number of products designed to make work in the kitchen easier and more fun. The ideas she shares and the products she shows in the next twenty minutes are from The Pampered Chef, a Chicago-area company that uses primarily the same home-show, or party-plan, system made famous by Tupperware.

Karen is one of the company's sales consultants. She was recently recruited by a neighbor who is a manager for the same firm. Karen has been doing home shows on some of her days off, but she has also been taking advantage of her new sales opportunity on flights as well.

By the end of this particular flight, she has taken orders for $340 in products and has earned herself about $85 in commissions.

* * *

Now we're in the busy office of a New York corporation, high above the Manhattan skyline. Denise, an executive secretary for a senior vice president, is happy because today is her "double payday." She has already received her weekly paycheck from the company—now she heads for a vacant office where she will meet several co-workers for lunch.

Most pack their sandwiches in bags; some bring in lunch from outside. But before they turn on the television to watch "All My Children," Denise distributes to her friends some fashion jewelry catalogs, samples of the jewelry, several necklaces, a bracelet, and a ring. They in turn give her their checks for the products.

Before the lunch hour is over, a few other people drop by, including a man from the mailroom, who has bought an anniversary gift for his wife, and a woman—a vice president—who has ordered a pearl necklace for herself.

You see, Denise is a part-time sales consultant for Lady Remington, and she likes those days when she is paid twice.

* * *

Holly Hedlund is a spokesperson at major trade shows in such places as McCormick Place in Chicago and Jacob Javits Center in New York. She represents Fortune 500 Companies such as Black and Decker, Amoco, and General Foods.

Holly's work calls for a glamorous image. She has that, but being an enterprising businesswoman of the 90s, she has taken another step toward the double payday. She is also an image consultant for Beauty Control, a rapidly growing direct-sales company based in Dallas, Texas. Her method of selling involves helping each client develop her best image, based on a number of factors including body type, facial shape, and personality.

The payoff is the sale of cosmetics and skin-care products. At a typical trade show, Holly finds herself surrounded by hundreds of other trade show reps, all of them looking for ways to enhance their images. Where could she find better prospects for her second career? Holly sells her contacts on the spot, schedules "image clinics" in their homes, or recruits them as salespeople—or all of the above. Direct selling is now her primary business. Her recruiting, accomplished primarily at trade shows, has enabled her to build a sales team of some ninety women.

YOUR CALLING CARD—SERVICE

Welcome to face-to-face selling in the 1990s. It promises to be a time of excitement, growth, and expansion for the direct-selling business—or for the *direct-service business,* depending on your point of view.

I like the term *direct service* as an alternative to *direct selling* because I'm convinced that the marketplace of the 90s craves *service.* If service is your calling card in this period, you'll have an "unfair advantage" in this marketplace, where a fast-food-merchandising mentality often predominates. It's a marketplace where the discount store salesperson often doesn't know or even care about the product that is being sold.

Direct selling is and will continue to be a powerful economic force in the United States. Nearly four million Americans are involved in direct selling to businesses and the public. Some 82 percent are women. Direct selling is a multibillion-dollar-a-year industry, totaling $9,695,095,000 in sales in 1988 (see Summary table) and, of course, growing.

The three scenarios described at the beginning of this chapter offer samples of how companies are reacting to today's changing sales environment. The examples show how selling in the workplace is becoming an increasingly important segment of direct selling.

How important? One billion, one hundred and thirty-four million dollars in sales in 1988—and on the rise.

That's important.

THINK ADVANTAGES

It has its advantages, this method of selling. It allows the salesperson to avoid some of the negative aspects of using more traditional methods. Some examples follow.

Finding the Prospect at Home The salesperson doesn't need to be concerned with catching a prospect at home. What's more, most people are more comfortable attending a sales

Summary: 1988 Direct Selling Industry Survey*

| Total 1988 Retail Sales: $9,695,556,000 |
| Total 1987 Retail Sales: $8,789,415,000 |

Percent of sales by major product groups:

Personal care products	33.7%
Home/Family care products	48.2%
Leisure/Educational products	8.2%
Services/Other	9.9%

Sales approach:

(method used to generate sales, reported as a percent of sales dollars)

One-on-one contact	79.0%
Group sales/Party plan	21.0%

Locus of sales:

In the home	In a workplace	Over the phone	At a public event**	Other
72.6%	11.7%	7.8%	3.0%	4.9%

| Total 1988 Salespeople: 3,996,067 |
| Total 1987 Salespeople: 3,614,038 |

Demographics of salespeople:

Independent	98.0%
Employed	2.0%
Full-time (30 + hours per wk)	19.4%
Part-time	80.6%
Male	18.6%
Female	81.4%

*From the Direct Selling Association, Washington, D.C.
**Such as a fair, exhibition, shopping mall, theme park, etc.

presentation in the workplace than allowing it in their own homes.

Affordability Well, you already know that all your prospects in the workplace are producing incomes, thereby increasing their ability to make buying decisions on their own.

I Don't Have Time Yes, everyone is busy these days; but buying products in the workplace actually saves customers time because it doesn't take any time out of a busy day or cost them any time searching for those items in a store after they leave work.

DEMOGRAPHIC FACTORS FOR THE 90S

There is no question that the marketplace is ever-changing, and nowhere is that more true than in the direct-selling field. Countless marketing studies have outlined the trends facing face-to-face sellers in the upcoming decade. Being aware of these trends and reacting to them is important to the successful face-to-face seller or service person.

This, however, is a sales book, not a marketing study, so I'll give you a summarization of a number of the studies and some of my thoughts on where the market is headed. Then we will get right into the *sales process*.

But first, a look at the marketplace as I see it!

"Family and social structures are changing. Dual career couples working are becoming the rule rather than the exception. Indeed, only one in ten North American families fits the traditional mold of the father at work and the mother at home with the kids."

Louis Harris Poll 1987

Working Women

More women than ever are entering the labor force, including those with families and young children, making it more difficult to find people at home during traditional working hours.

Number of Families with Children

The number of families with children is on the rise as the "echo of the baby boom" goes into full swing.

Smaller Families

At the same time, the average family size is growing smaller; the great majority of families will have one or two children, while fewer and fewer families will have three or more children. Families with many children will be practically unheard of.

Lack of Time

The "baby boomers" coming into middle age are used to buying quality. They like quality merchandise, and they like their quality time. They do not like to waste time, and they make relatively quick buying decisions.

It is easy to understand why time is so important to the buyer. "The trend is toward longer working hours and less leisure," says Louis Harris. "The average work week has risen to 49 hours from 41 hours in 1973, an increase of 20 percent in 15 years. The average amount of leisure time has decreased by 32 percent in the same period."

Spendable Income

While both parents working means a boom for the day-care business and makes it difficult to find people at home, disposable income will be much higher than before.

Two breadwinners plus fewer children in the home equals more spendable dollars for a family. Women are much freer in their purchase decisions when they have their own incomes. Women will also be much more amenable to trying part-time vocations, such as the ones available in the direct-selling field.

Alternative Ways of Buying

People in the 90s will continue to be much more amenable to buying through the mail or buying direct. They do not want to waste time searching through stores, trying to find what they want, dealing with often unknowledgeable clerks. Because their time is much more valuable these days, they like the idea of shopping in the comfort of their homes, either over the phone, via television, through a catalog, or face-to-face with a friend or acquaintance. (On this point, I was interested to read the other day that one car firm is trying to sell automobiles door-to-door. They have been frustrated by the traditional means of doing business and are now going direct to customers with their offers. Whether or not this approach succeeds, it is definitely a trend; and it's a trend that I'm excited about because it's another indication that skills developed in *Face-to-Face Selling* are always going to be valuable.)

Over-the-Counter vs. Face-to-Face Selling

Over-the-counter shopping at malls or fairs will continue to blossom. Many impulsive shoppers feel comfortable walking through a mall, and when they see a display for products or services traditionally sold door-to-door, they will spend several hundred dollars with a charge card—quickly and easily.

Special Offers

The marketing approach that uses an "offer" will become unbelievably sophisticated in the upcoming decade. People are no longer fooled by direct solicitations with their names on them now that they know computerized machines can crank out "personalized" letters by the ton. Alternative means of grabbing the reader's or viewer's attention will be developed.

Older Buyers

Grandparents and other "golden agers" will make up one of the most lucrative purchasing groups in the history of the nation. The number of people over sixty will continue to soar, and they will have lots and lots of expendable dollars, a lot of which they'll more than likely spend on their grandchildren as well as themselves.

Technology

The use of the fax will continue to grow as a means of communication, billing, even selling, but you can expect it to be tightly controlled. It may never be seriously utilized as a means of selling.

I'm reminded of the commercial on television for an airline that shows a businessman talking to his sales force, telling them they must all have "face-to-face contacts" with their customers in the upcoming weeks. His advice was initiated by an old friend who had fired the businessman's company that morning because of a lack of attentiveness to the account. He says, "We used to do business with a handshake, now we do it by fax." But neither the fax nor the computer will ever replace face-to-face contact as a means of selling. Both, however, will be important in the 1990s selling picture.

Selling in the Workplace

As the examples at the beginning of the chapter pointed out, selling in the workplace will become an even greater phenomenon than it already is. Look for companies to offer "swap" sessions in which they'll group-sell to each other's employees over lunch. Also look for deals to be consummated that allow people to sell products and services in company cafeterias.

GREATER OPPORTUNITIES

What all this means for the direct-selling industry is that opportunities will be greater than ever before, but our methods will become more sophisticated. Working women will contribute both as consumers with disposable income and as potential representatives. Women are rejoining the work force in droves. Where are these women coming from? Some will come right out of college, some will have already been working, but the greatest number will come from one group in particular—women returning to the work force.

This group is composed of women who have graduated from or left college a few years ago, were married, worked for a while, and then left the labor force to have children. As those children grow older and enter school, these women—often bright, talented, and with degrees—will return in some capacity to the labor force. Many will take part-time positions, often accepting salaries much lower than they had earned prior to leaving their old jobs.

For the direct-service industry, these women represent a rich pool of new recruits. Why will these women be attracted to the direct-selling field? Sales is a growing field in general for women, and not just the direct-service area.

According to Peter D. Bennett in his book, *Marketing* (McGraw-Hill, NY, 1988), a nationwide survey of 1,400 salespeople under the age of thirty revealed that one-third are women, 63 percent are college graduates, 11 percent hold MBA degrees, and less than 2 percent have no college training.

Bennett reports that one company (Brown & Bigelow) had no women on its sales force until the 70s and that, by 1985, 25 percent of the company's salesforce were women. I'm sure that Bennett's survey is talking about full-time, traditional, salaried sales positions outside the typical direct-service area.

On the downside: In corporations, despite the growing numbers of women in sales positions, these same women are finding it difficult to gain the respect accorded their male colleagues. Bennett cites Dr. Barbara Pletcher of the National Association of Professional Saleswomen, who suggests that a saleswoman's expertise is often questioned or challenged. In the direct-selling field, such attitudes are practically unheard of. That's another reason why a sales position in a direct-sales company—with its unlimited income potential and the opportunity to be your own boss—can be more attractive to these returning female professionals. It probably accounts for the statistic we saw earlier, that 82 percent of all the salespeople in the Direct Selling Association (DSA) are women.

So, how will direct-selling people prepare themselves to enter this marketplace? First, by remembering that it is a *direct service* business and therefore requires giving their prospects and customers more service than they could get elsewhere.

Second, by continuing to practice and becoming efficient in the basics. The fundamentals are always going to be key selling skills, product knowledge, and the ability to find prospects.

Also necessary will be a more sophisticated approach to the overall marketing functions of our business. By this I mean total service in terms of meeting the needs of your customers on an ongoing and permanent basis.

A research study by The Forum Corporation, cited in the April 1989 issue of *The Training and Developmental Journal,* concluded that "selling now involves much more than taking an order and arranging a payment schedule." That approach, says the report, is outmoded but remains common. Forum asserts that salespeople who continue to rely on "hit and run" techniques "ignore current thinking that sales productivity requires a partnership between buyer and seller. Even more important, they ignore the fact that successful salespeople now play many different roles."

Yes, the role of the salesperson is more complicated, but it really gets down to inspiring a basic trust and faith in you, as a person. When you are selling a product or service, you are selling yourself more than anything else. If you can do that, you'll be successful.

BUILD RELATIONSHIPS

I liked what the chief executive of COMDISCO, a billion-dollar-a-year Chicago computer leasing outfit, said about his company's sales philosophy in a 1987 *Fortune* magazine article. Kenneth N. Pontikes said: "The way to win is to build long-term relationships instead of chasing transactions." He recruited the best salespeople he could find and instructed them not to hustle for sales. "Just let the people get to know us," he said. He was talking about selling yourself before you sell your product. It works.

Having discussed the marketplace of the 90s, let's look at the financial rewards that part- or full-time positions offer in the direct-selling business.

Stories about personal experiences can best illustrate what face-to-face selling will offer you in the 90s. You may be wondering, is this decade really the time of *unlimited opportunity* in face-to-face selling?

Ask Joan Henning, sales director for Longaberger Baskets of Zanesville, Ohio. Joan lives in a Chicago suburb. Her income exceeds $100,000 per year and is still going up.

Opportunity for the 90s?

Ask Nicholas Barsan, who emigrated from Romania in 1968 and became a convert to capitalism. According to *Fortune* Magazine, he was making more than $1 million a year selling real estate when *Fortune* interviewed him.

Ask Jan Gilmore, now a top sales manager for *World Book Encyclopedia* in California, whose income exceeded $460,000 last year. Jan came to the United States from Australia in the late 1970s.

SUMMARY

Sure, the people we have just mentioned are stars. They *worked* to get where they are in sales. But *anyone* can do it— *anyone* can make not only good but great money in sales in this decade.

My own company may be small, but it's a good example. Our salespeople, if they are willing to work hard, usually earn $30 or more an hour. That's at the very beginning, before they move into managerial positions. After that, gangbusters.

The figures don't lie. Even in this field where your financial rewards are in direct proportion to the results you get, the returns are eyebrow-raising. This applies across the board, both to those companies that belong to the Direct Selling Association and to all others in direct selling.

Later in this book you'll find out how much you can expect to make if you go into direct selling. You'll want to take the variables into account, of course; nothing is uniform from company to company. But they have one element in common:

They'll give you a chance to *make it big!* ❏

CHAPTER TWO

The Art of Creative Confrontation

've been practicing what I call "the art of creative confrontation" for over twenty-five years now. I've decided it's time to pass along to others some useful things I've learned.

When I sat down and really thought about it, I realized that the most important skill successful salespeople (and successful people in general) have is not the gift of gab, or an engaging personality, or a winning smile. It's the ability to deal with others effectively through creative confrontation. People who succeed in selling are almost always masters of this art. Yet I know it isn't necessarily something you're born with. You can learn it!

DOES "CONFRONTATION" SOUND TOO MENACING?

Don't let my term "creative confrontation" give you the wrong impression. Some people think a confrontation has to be an angry, hostile scene with a lot of yelling and screaming. It doesn't. Actually, I think most of the yelling and screaming that people do are attempts to avoid a confrontation with the truth—about themselves or about some part of their lives that isn't working for them.

Facing Things Boldly

Webster defines the term "confront" as "to face things boldly." And that's exactly the way I mean it. In all my years in selling face-to-face, the biggest winners I've known have been the ones who knew how to face things boldly. Not with bluster or hostility, but with courage and determination. They came to grips with each situation they faced. That's what makes a confrontation "creative." And that's the only kind of confrontation I'm interested in.

Case No. 1 Consider the following: I was selling advertising space. A prospective client, the owner of a $10 million business, was reluctant to come to the phone when I called him. Even when he did, he sounded hostile from the first word.

"I'm busy," he said, "very busy. I doubt if I'm interested. You can stop by if you want, but I can't guarantee you anything. Do what you want. But I warn you, you're probably wasting your time." I knew, however, that he was someone who could benefit from my product.

When I got to his office, his secretaries—plural—were reserved but pleasant. "He's very busy," one of them told me, "but would you like a cup of coffee?" I would, and I did.

After a few minutes, Mr. Abrasive came out, looked me over, and said, "I see you got coffee. Why didn't you order breakfast?"

"I didn't want to push my luck," I replied, thinking how much I'd really like to up and walk out on this turkey (most inexperienced salespeople would have). But I was already applying the art of creative confrontation. He disappeared into his office. And I waited.

Finally, the Boss came out again, saw that I was still there, and said grimly, "Okay, you've got about five minutes."

At this point, I sensed that he knew I wasn't intimidated by his bluster. I had taken the right stance. In doing so, I had told him that I had something to sell that he needed. He invited me into his inner sanctum.

To make a long story short, twenty minutes later I had closed the sale and had an invitation to lunch. Without the "art of creative confrontation," I might never have gotten into his office. By facing things boldly and taking the right stance, I had done what I had come to do.

Lesson: Often the prospect who is toughest to sell may become your strongest supporter. This was such a situation.

Within a year, Mr. Abrasive (who turned into Mr. Nice Guy) flew me at his own expense to a company golf outing in another city.

Case No. 2 Need more proof? In another case, Pat Chevako, selling for *World Book,* got to a sales appointment only to find that the lady of the house was down with the flu.

Pat, a sensitive, discerning soul, asked herself: "Go or no go?" She decided to go, and went ahead into the sickroom as her normal, bouncy, enthusiastic self.

The sickroom was the living room. Mrs. Jones (not her real name) was lying on the couch with a cold pack on her forehead. Pat greeted her, expressed sympathy, and asked, "Is this a good time?"

"No time is a good time," said Mrs. Jones, "but please go ahead."

Pat went ahead. During her presentation, she had no idea whether Mrs. Jones was listening or not. When she had finished, Mrs. Jones called in a loud voice, "Susie, will you bring me my checkbook?" Susie brought it, and Mrs. Jones wrote a check for the entire range of *World Book* products.

A few weeks later, Pat received a note from Mrs. Jones. "Pat," it said, "I thought I'd write to say a personal thank-you for bringing a ray of sunshine into my life on that dreary day last month. Your zest and enthusiasm was better medicine for my flu than what the doctor had given me. Equally important, Susie and I have been enjoying the *World Book* since the day it arrived."

The Goal of Every Creative Confrontation

Your goal will vary with the nature of the confrontation. If you're in sales—and you probably are if you're reading this book—your goal is the sale. But whether you're selling or not, the goal is always *to resolve the situation to your satisfaction.*

The Five Rules of Creative Confrontation

To become a master of this priceless art, be sure to practice each of these five rules very carefully:

1) *Maintain the right STANCE.*

2) *Keep your COOL.*

3) *Be PREPARED with facts.*

4) *Use your COMMON SENSE.*

5) *Let the other person keep his or her DIGNITY.*

We will discuss each of these rules in detail, but first let me make a couple of other points.

The first creative confrontation you need to have is with yourself.

Never forget that "If you're not satisfied with your progress, the person responsible is always available for consultation." That's you. The face that stares back at you from the bathroom mirror each morning is the most important person in your life. And one of your most important lifelong tasks is to get to know that person—charms, talents, warts, and all. The better you know that person, the better your chances of getting the kind of performance you want out of him or her. So face that bathroom mirror boldly.

The most important creative confrontation is with yourself.

Your second creative confrontation is with the new day ahead.

Every twenty-four hours, you get a new chance to "face things boldly." Shrink from this challenge, and you waste another day. Apply the art of creative confrontation, and something good will happen.

Many people overlook the fact that each day breaks down, quite naturally, into little pieces—each one an opportunity for a creative confrontation. For the dentist, each segment is a patient. For the student, each piece is a class. For the salesperson, each piece is a selling opportunity.

Life never stops giving us another chance—another opportunity to "face things boldly."

Ask yourself: What are the important pieces of my day? They are the confrontations that can lead you to success—if you *use them creatively to resolve each situation to your satisfaction.*

You can do it if you want to.

Learn creative confrontation and you can even fire someone and still be friends.

Some situations seem crafted for disaster. Right?

Wrong!

How about firing someone?

I was on a flight from Pennsylvania to Chicago. The strapping young fellow in the seat next to me had been dropped by the Washington Redskins football team that very day and was on his way back home to the western part of the United States. Although he was really disappointed about not making the team he couldn't say enough about the Redskins' organization, its coaches and its management.

Why? Mostly because he had had a good experience during his time in camp, but maybe more importantly, because of the way they had "confronted" him about not making the team. He told me that the general manager assured him he had the talent to play in the NFL—he admired both his athletic ability and his attitude—but unfortunately the team was caught in a situation where they simply had too many good athletes who could play his position.

The young athlete contrasted that treatment to that of a previous team that had given him a tryout.

His feeling toward the other team and its coaches was one of bitterness. The major difference was the quality of the *"selling job."*

The additional expenditure on the part of the Redskins for the goodwill was probably twenty minutes of the general manager's time spent in practicing the art of creative confrontation.

This reminded me of an experience I had some years ago when I was in charge of a large national sales force. I had the rather unpleasant task of firing a highly paid sales manager. Even though I liked the guy and got along with him well on a personal level, his performance simply did not justify retaining him.

I invited him into my office to tell him. Also attending the meeting was his immediate supervisor, a vice president of the company.

Remember the rules.

Now the important thing in any situation like this is to remember those *Five Rules of Creative Confrontation*. First, the STANCE I took with him was friendly and respectful. Second, I kept my COOL—there was no point, after all, in getting angry. Third, I was well PREPARED with facts that supported my decision. (Actually, I never had to use them; he knew.) Fourth, I used my COMMON SENSE in my whole discussion with the man—and appealed to his. Fifth, I never once questioned his innate talent and ability, so I allowed him to retain his DIGNITY.

The interesting thing about this experience was that the man left our "exit interview" in good spirits, determined to move on to better things and without anger or bitterness toward me or the sales organization.

He was so jovial, in fact, that his boss asked me, "Are you sure he knows he's been fired?" The VP, a "blood and guts" type, had assumed that the interview should be a "chewing out," marked by personal attack and defense and ending in bitterness and hostility. It didn't happen that way—it didn't have to because I made a point of practicing the art of creative confrontation.

So, you see, creative confrontation skills can be valuable to you in selling a product or in selling a person on accepting your way of thinking. The style you choose in "facing things boldly" should be tailored to the situation.

Often, it means knowing "how to step on someone's shoes without messing up their shine."

A Look at the Five Rules in More Detail

1) *STANCE*   Although my philosophy is not as cynical as that expressed in the best-selling book *Winning Through Intimidation,* I have to admit that I got a message from it that had a strong impact on me: "The outcome of every personal encounter depends to a great extent on the psychological stance you bring to that encounter." If you feel less than equal to the other party, you have a problem. If you feel that other party will outtalk, outsmart, or outmaneuver you, you again have a problem.

One of the best real estate salespersons I know showed a parcel of land that was actually one segment of a large estate. The prospects seemed interested but thought the price was too high. The salesperson responded by telling the prospects that four other similar pieces of land had sold at comparable prices, and he pointed out why this property was in the same ball park—the type of house, the picturesque rural setting, and so on. Then he said he would be leaving town on Monday, but that if the prospects were still interested, they could call him at home over the weekend. At that point he stopped selling.

His *stance* was this: I've given you all the basic details, and now you have to make up your own minds.

By telling the prospects about his Monday departure, he had left them with two things: 1) a sense of urgency that they had better make a decision and get to him before Monday; and 2) the feeling that it didn't matter to him that much if they bought the land or not—that it was well worth the price and that he'd probably have another buyer waiting when he got back from his trip.

Needless to say, the prospects called Sunday night and he got the sale. His *stance* had been exactly right.

2) *COOL*   This is a matter of staying relaxed, no matter what happens. Your prospect will be more relaxed if you are. (We've all heard of the person who doesn't *have* ulcers but is a *carrier.)*

Suppose the prospect says, "No, I don't want any of the household items you're selling. They don't go with my decor." You answer, calmly, "Quite right, they don't. I see you like modern furnishings. I'd like to show you our line of decorative pieces that would go beautifully with the way you've styled your home. I can get you practically anything you need."

In other words, *don't panic when you hear the word "no."* It's often more a challenge than a refusal. Stay cucumber-cool, positive, and helpful. *Never feel you've been put down.*

How do you know when a *no* really means *NO?*

We'll have much more on this later. But it's important to remember that creative confrontation is logical. It's based on the fact that few prospects simply say no and mean it as a final answer. Most often, they are arguing the merits of your proposal in their heads. You want to remain helpful.

And if you're convinced that a *no* means *NO? Stop selling to that person or group.*

3) *PREPARED*   In a later chapter, I want to go into detail about the importance of having a well-prepared sales talk. At this point, let me just say that every-

thing you do will go better if you do your homework first.

If you're selling wines, know what foods they go with best, how long they have aged, the temperatures they should be served at. A lot of the selling you do is guiding people through unfamiliar territory. Make sure you know the way yourself!

4) *COMMON SENSE* Some call it "traditional wisdom." It's my favorite way of avoiding the booby traps that every sales situation is strewn with.

What booby traps? Well, suppose you and the prospect find you have a mutual acquaintance—someone you personally don't care for very much. Resist the temptation to tell the prospect you think the other guy is a jerk. The prospect may consider him a good friend. Let your common sense make certain you keep your opinions to yourself.

5) *DIGNITY* I once knew a salesman who eventually turned to bus driving for a living. His problem had been that he just couldn't resist "putting a prospect in his or her place" if they didn't agree with him. He'd say, "That other stuff you bought won't work. You wasted your money on it."

In effect, he was telling his prospects they didn't know how to manage their own affairs. He kept chipping away at their dignity until they wanted to throw him out.

Most of All, Have the Right Stance

Is any one of the five rules of creative confrontation more important than the others?

Of the five, the *stance* you take is the most important of all. Decide that you are in control, and things will fall into place.

SUMMARY

Starting no later than the moment you look into the bathroom mirror tomorrow morning, make each new encounter a creative confrontation. Face each one boldly and, this I promise, you will amaze yourself with the results. ❏

CHAPTER THREE

Turning Stumbling-Blocks into Stepping-Stones

et's suppose you know your product. And you understand the basic principles of making your presentation. But something is holding you back. Maybe it's inertia, excuses, fear, imaginary problems. Maybe it's all of the above. But something is keeping you from having the success you want.

The problem is not uncommon—especially in people who are just starting a career in sales. In fact, I've known many beginners who were all fired up with enthusiasm but who, six months later, were out of business. Trouble is, they don't understand why. Some mysterious "something" held them back—kept them from realizing all they had hoped for.

Well, fear not. I've run into a few of these mysterious "somethings" myself. I call them "stumbling-blocks." And, over the years, I've used the art of creative confrontation to turn them into "stepping-stones" to success.

SEVEN OF THE WORST

Let's look at some of these stumbling-blocks and see how you can stop *stumbling* over them and start *stepping* on them. Here's what seven of the worst sound like:

1. *"I'm just not a born salesperson!"*
2. *"I don't have enough time to do it!"*
3. *"I don't know enough yet!"*
4. *"I don't want to have to sell to my friends!"*
5. *"I don't know who to call on!"*
6. *"I can't seem to get out of my own door!"*
7. *"I'm no good at handling rejection!"*

These are seven of the stumbling-blocks I've seen many times over the years. Now, let's see how you can have a creative confrontation with any or all of them.

Great salespeople are not born—they're made.

1. "I'm just not a born salesperson!"

I don't know who dreamed up the idea we're all born a certain way and can't change a thing about it. But they did a terrible disservice to humanity.

The truth is, salespeople are *made,* not born. This is an absolute, indisputable *fact.* I know it is. I've seen hundreds who got off to miserable starts and later turned into fabulously successful people—the kind that new people, just entering the business, would describe as "natural-born salespeople!"

A Chapter 3 Thought

Half the failures in life arise from pulling in one's horse as he is leaping.

J. C. and A. W. Hare

I know of one psychologist, responsible for selecting candidates for sales careers, who says that any "effective person" can learn to sell. By "effective person," he means anyone who has: a) a mature personality; b) some stick-to-it-iveness; and c) the ability to function in the world.

"I try to establish in interviews and tests whether the person is effective in a general way," he says. "If the answer is positive and no other problems appear, the candidate stands a good chance to succeed." He doesn't say a single word about any "magical gift."

"I wonder if I could succeed in selling."

Studies show that more than half the population has wondered, at some time or another, if they could be successful in a selling career. *More than half!* And, chances are, there's a very good reason why so many people do so much wondering: It's called money.

Now there is no doubt that a successful career in selling can often mean big money in a relatively short time—even for someone without a college degree or any special social status to begin with. So wondering is a pretty good place to start. Just don't be one of the ones who do a little wondering, only to conclude, "Oh, no, not me. I'd never be able to do it!"

Don't sell yourself short!

The worst kind of prejudice you can have is prejudice against *yourself*. You don't have to be a "born salesperson" or a born anything. Give yourself a break. Here's how:

1) *Remind yourself that doing a salesperson's job simply means bringing a product or service together with someone who is a prospect for it.*

   You take a product that does something for people. And you find someone who needs to have something done. And then you show the prospect the product.

   I don't mean to oversimplify. But that, in essence, is all selling really is. Keep that in mind.

2) *Remember that thousands have done it before you.* Most selling jobs have already been done successfully by others. You don't have to reinvent the wheel. "Buy the package" of the company you're selling for—their training programs, their sales approach, their sales system—and put it to work. If others are making "the system" work, you can too.

3) *Always remember "Rockbottom John"!* He was in his mid-thirties when I met him, and it really did seem that he had hit rock bottom. He had lost his production control job at a nearby plant. Almost immediately after that, his wife, a registered nurse, lost her job. To make matters worse, the strain of it all was getting to both of them, and the marriage was in trouble.

   In desperation, John decided to "try" selling. He applied, was hired, and spent the first day with a manager who happened to be particularly good with sales recruits. The manager took the time to make several very effective presentations to show John how it was done. Then he said, "Now you try it." And John did.

The results were remarkable. Following the example of the sales manager, John succeeded in closing his first sale. Little by little, a major change began to come over him. His worried, frazzled look gave way to a broad grin of pleasure as he realized that, for the first time in long while, he was going to have a day when things went right.

"Rockbottom John" never went back to production control. His income from selling soon topped his old job by far. His marital situation improved, and, when he looked back on the day he lost his job at the plant, it seemed to him it had been his "lucky day." It had, after all, led him to a brand-new career. His experience proved that in every adversity lies the seed of success.

2. "I don't have enough time to do it!"

A lot of people have said it: "I need the money . . . I like the product . . . I like the way the company sells the product. If only I had time, I could be a big success!"

To which I reply with an old adage: "If you want something done, get a busy person to do it!" If you really want to do something, the time is always there.

How much time do you have for anything, anyway? How much time does anyone have? Well, there are 24 hours in a day and 7 days in a week. Multiply 24 by 7 and you get 168 hours in a week. Let's suppose you work full-time and you sleep about the same amount of time as most other people. Here's what it looks like:

Hours in a week	168
Hours spent working	40
Hours spent sleeping	56
TOTAL TIME LEFT OVER	72

So you've got 72 hours a week left after you take care of the main essentials. Okay, life is full of obligations—to spouse, friends, church, hobbies, home. But let's be honest, a good chunk of those 72 hours just dribbles away. Put just 10 percent of it to work for you in sales, and you have the equivalent of a full working day each week in front of your prospects! That's just one-tenth of your discretionary time.

Remember that your free time isn't really "free."

How much can you make in an hour? Twelve dollars? Twenty-five? Forty? A hundred? That's what it costs you for each hour spent slumped in front of the TV. Remember that.

And remember something else: old habits may seem to die hard, but actually it only takes about thirty days to grow a new one. So decide what "free" activity you can do without, and plan to use that time, every week for the next month, to get in a little more selling. Try it, and a month from now, you'll feel a lot better about everything!

Two coffee breaks a day may cost you thirty minutes daily. That's one hundred fifty minutes in a five-day week. Seventy-eight hundred minutes a year. One hundred thirty hours. *Three and one-half weeks a year.*

Did you know Herbert Hoover once wrote a book in ninety days? He did it entirely by scribbling while he rode a daily commuter train.

You know the secret? You "gotta wanna!" Wanting is everything.

3. *"I don't know enough yet!"*

I've heard it so many times: "I don't know enough about this business yet. I'm something of a perfectionist. When I do something, I want to do it well. As soon as I've done all the studying I need to do, I'll go out and become a big success!"

Let me remind you of three things:

1. Everyone makes mistakes. Cardinal Cushing once said, "Nothing in the world would be accomplished if we waited until we could do it so well that we would never make a mistake!" Believe me, you can make mistakes and survive to tell the tale. I'm living proof of that.

2. Action cures fear. Saying you don't know enough sometimes means you just lack the guts to try. You're chicken. And the funny thing about being chicken is that you can often overcome it if you'll just do something. I know. I've been chicken myself a few times.

3. The prospect knows even less than you do. Most prospects can't tell how ignorant you are because when it comes to your product, they're even more ignorant than you.

Most prospects assume you know everything anyone needs to know about your product. If they ask something you can't answer, don't panic. Admit you don't know the answer, promise to get it, then go get it and bring it back. Turn your knowledge gap into a positive, sales-producing opportunity.

Who Cares If You Mess Up?

If you mess up, so what? Most things in life simply aren't the big deals we think they are at the time.

Several years ago I went to watch my son play in a high school basketball game. He did well, I thought, and his team won the game. Afterwards, I went over to congratulate the victors. As I approached my son, however, I noticed he was upset. "Oh, Dad," he groaned, "did you see that air ball? I can't believe I did that. What a klutz!"

I had absolutely no idea what he was talking about. Then he reminded me of a particular incident during the game. Though I recalled the play, I hadn't recognized it as an "air ball" at all. I thought he had deliberately passed the ball to a teammate, who had, in fact, scored immediately. I had assumed the whole play was deliberate, and so, I'm sure, almost all the fans did, too.

To my son, his minor and meaningless blooper was a major embarrassment. It didn't need to be. Probably no one else had even noticed.

4. "I Don't Want to Have to Sell to My Friends!"

Some salespeople—especially those new to the business—fear that friends will consider them high-pressure nuisances if they try to sell them anything. Let me tell you something: This particular stumbling-block is often the biggest stepping-stone of all.

They Deserve to Know

Got a good product? Are you proud of it? Then your friends deserve to hear about it, don't they? After all, I'm sure that you're excited about your product or you wouldn't have decided to sell it. If your friends really don't need it, they can say no. But what if they buy a similar product from someone else and then come to you later and say, "I really needed it, but I didn't know I could get it from you. Why didn't you tell me?"

Throughout my career, I have often heard about this kind of thing happening, usually with beginning salespeople who might have been a bit gun-shy. These salespeople would come to me, furious with themselves, and say, "I can't believe I was so dumb! My friend just bought the competitor's product—the one that's so much more expensive—and now they tell me they'd have preferred our product if only they'd known I was selling it!"

The worst part of a situation like this is that it makes you look as though you're not proud of what you're doing. So your friends will hesitate to tell other friends what you're doing because they think you're trying to hide it. Furthermore, one lost sales opportunity may really mean you've lost a bunch of sales to a whole "nest" of possible customers.

Every single person you know—even a "nodding acquaintance"—sits at the center of a circle of friends, relatives, co-workers, and business associates, any one of whom may be an excellent prospect for what you have to sell.

Practice Your Presentation with Friends

A great way to let friends in on what you're doing is to ask them to let you practice your sales talk on them. Ask them to be your "guinea pigs," then do the best job you can. You'll get some sales and probably some referrals, too. (This technique works especially well in party-plan selling—see chapter 11, "Group Selling.") Make it seem as if your party is a "dry run." Then watch the sales pour in!

A New Career?

Practicing your presentation with friends, you may introduce one or more of them to a new career in sales. It's happened more often than you might think. In fact, your friends and relatives may include some great recruiting prospects, and—since most companies reward you handsomely for bringing in new sales recruits—you may reap a double benefit.

Enthusiasm is always infectious. If your product is good, you aren't imposing on anyone by telling them *how* good. And remember that even the last friend in the world probably won't buy something just because it's you who happens to be selling it—especially if it costs more than a few dollars. And if it's a little-ticket item, they aren't risking much if they do buy one.

5. *"I don't know who to call on!"*

If you're applying good prospecting techniques, you'll always have someone to call on. Yet—year in and year out—I've heard this complaint.

Prospecting is so important, I've devoted the whole of Chapter 6 to it. So we'll come to the details later. Meanwhile, let me tell you a couple of stories.

The Night Before and the Man Next Door

This story was told to me some years ago by a wonderfully successful salesperson. When he was just getting started in sales, he found himself lying awake one night, wondering if he was going to make it. He kept tossing and turning and worrying and fretting. Finally, his thrashing about woke his wife, who wanted to know what was keeping him so restless. He told her.

"Listen," she said, "get up right now and write who you're going to call on tomorrow morning. Then get some sleep so you'll be fresh and awake enough to make the call."

He followed her advice and, mercifully, drifted off to sleep. Next morning, he took the piece of paper he had left on his dresser, called his prospect, and made an appointment.

Feeling better about everything, he drove across town to meet his prospect and ran into a disappointment. "I'm terribly sorry," said the receptionist, "but Mr. Smith was called away unexpectedly. He won't be back until tomorrow. He asked me to call you and reschedule, but you'd already left."

Looking very downcast, the salesman thanked the receptionist. Suddenly, she jumped up. "Hold on a minute," she said. "As long as you're here, maybe you ought to talk to the company next door. I have a feeling they might be in the market for your product. Tell Marge, the receptionist, that I said I thought it might be a good idea if she could get her boss to talk to you for a minute or two!"

So next door he went. And Marge got him in to see Mr. Brown, her boss. And what do you think happened? He got the sale, plus three referrals that turned into customers that same day, plus a new appointment to see his original prospect the next day.

When he got home with that "good, tired, feeling," that evening, the first thing he did was give his wife a big hug for her moral support and her excellent idea. The second thing he did was take a piece of paper and write on it, "The night before and the man next door."

As this salesman finished his story, he opened his wallet and took out the piece of paper. It was kind of yellow and crumpled. But the words he had written on it years before summed up his whole philosophy of selling: Always be sure you have a prospect to see the next day. And never walk away from that sales call without prospecting next door! And that's how a sleepless night turned into a brilliantly successful career!

The moral of the story is that although the hardest door to get through is your own, it's a lot easier to get through it if you've got some place to go. Even if that doesn't work out, there's probably another opportunity as good or better nearby.

The Swing and the Tricycle

I once knew a sales trainer who told me about one particular trainee he took out on the road one day. The trainee wanted to drive, drive, drive, it seemed, and after a call at a private home, he said to the trainer, "Let's go! I've got another prospect on the other side of town."

"One second," said the trainer. "Your market is families with young children, right?" "Right," said the trainee. "Well," said the trainer, "look at that house next door. What do you see in the yard?"

The trainee looked. "Er, a swing set and a tricycle."

"Yes," said the trainer, "and while it's possible the adults may occasionally use the swing set, there's not much chance they get a lot of use out of the tricycle. So what does that tell you?"

"Kids," said the trainee. "They must have kids."

"Right," said the trainer. "And that makes them prospects. So, before we go driving all across town, let's stop in next door and see what happens!" So they did. And made another sale.

6. "I can't seem to get out of my own door!"

It's true: The hardest door to get through is your own. But if you'll just grab yourself by the collar and force your way through that one, all the other doors will be much easier! In fact, I've always found that it's much easier to stay out than to get out. Isn't that nice to know, when you really think about it? It means you get rid of the hard part first!

At Least Put Your Hat On!

One of the greatest salespeople I've ever met tells me that when she gets up in the morning, the first thing she does is put her hat on. "I always feel a little silly," she says, "walking around with my hat on. And the sillier I feel, the more anxious I am to finish dressing, eat my breakfast and start my day! In fact, I just can't wait to get out of the house!"

Get to Work on Time!

Salespeople usually don't punch timeclocks. You're your own boss. If you're good, you can make five or six times the money most clock-punchers make. But being good usually means getting to work on time—even if there's no clock to punch and no boss to check up on you and frown at his watch if you're late.

7. "I'm no good at handling rejection!"

I've heard it so often. "What if they say no?" "What if they're rude to me and tell me to go away!" "What if they give me the message that I'm bothering them?" "What if I tramp around to prospect after prospect and nobody buys a darn thing?" "I don't think I can stand feeling like a loser over and over again."

Of course it's human to want to be accepted, not rejected. But hearing someone say "No" doesn't make you a loser. Not at all. I promise you, I've heard the word thousands of times myself. Often, it's just a phase you go through on your way to "Maybe" and eventually to "Yes."

Let me explain some important things I've learned about rejection.

It's Nothing Personal

When someone declares, very firmly, that he or she absolutely does not want to buy your product, it almost never means they're rejecting you personally. In fact, they may have quite enjoyed chatting with you.

To some people, a friendly, enthusiastic salesperson can be a breath of fresh air in an otherwise boring day. It may be that they would love to have your product, even though they don't indicate that to you. They may simply be unable to afford it. The timing may be bad for them, financially. They may have other commitments or problems that force them to refuse your product even though they may be sorely tempted.

What I want you to understand is that when someone says, "No, thank you, it's not for me," that doesn't mean, "You are a terrible, obnoxious person and I want you out of my sight right now!" So don't take it that way.

Home Run Hitters Strike Out a Lot!

Two of the greatest home run hitters of all time, Babe Ruth and Hank Aaron, are also among the strikeout leaders in the history of baseball. Lots of successes often go along with lots of failures. On your way to a lot of "Yes's," you may well set a world record for "No's." Consider yourself lucky and laugh all the way to the bank.

The Luxury of Being "Down"

I remember a regional sales manager who was quite concerned about one of his salespeople. "Sally is so down these days," he said. "I know she was hoping to be a sales manager herself by now, and she's disappointed."

"Well," I said, "if she wants to be a sales manager, she can't afford the luxury of being down." The manager passed this comment along to Sally, who had the good sense to think it over and perk up. Eventually, she got what she wanted.

A man I know, now president of a major company, recalled the early years of his career. At one point, he had wanted to quit his job and his boss had asked him why.

"I haven't been to college," he replied, "and I'm no good at public speaking."

"So what will changing jobs do for you?" asked the manager. "If you're no good at public speaking in this job, you'll be no good at public speaking in your next job. Why don't you stay here and work on your public speaking skills?" And he did.

SUMMARY

In this chapter, I've tried to give you some concrete examples of "the art of creative confrontation" in action: how you can use it to turn stumbling-blocks into stepping-stones. One of the most important things to remember is that most of these stumbling-blocks are just human fears and frailties that you can overcome by changing your attitude.

We're all subject to fears and frailties—even people who seem to be on top of everything. Early in my sales career, I remember hearing Charlie Jones, author of *Life is Tremendous,* as a guest speaker.

At one point, Charlie said, "We all think we're unique. We think we're the only ones who are worried about something. We're not. For example, right now I'm up here trying to make a good impression on Bart."

I was at a lower level of management at the time, and Charlie Jones was a successful, well-known, and widely respected speaker. I had been trying to make a good impression on *him,* and it amazed me that he would even bother to try to impress *me!*

So don't worry. You're not alone. We all stumble. Just practice the art of creative confrontation and turn all your stumbling-blocks into stepping-stones. ❏

CHAPTER FOUR

Goal Setting
and the Five P's

I was serving as sales manager in Pennsylvania. With our entire sales team really producing, we enjoyed a fabulous week.

I got a call from the sales manager in the New York office. "Bart, how in the heck did your team do it? What's the secret?" "No secret," I replied. "We just set some goals and we met them."

"Goals?" he laughed. He just couldn't believe that the simple act of setting goals and working diligently to meet them could be the cause of our spectacular performance. He seemed to think I was hiding something I didn't want to share with him. I wasn't.

I had willingly shared the "secret" of our success. And I'll willingly share it with you now.

Two Things Goals Do For You

Set yourself some sensible, achievable goals, and, this I promise, they'll help you in at least the following two ways:

First, they supply you with a handy reminder of where you want to go. At any given moment, and especially if you feel you may be straying off track a little, they bring you back into focus.

Second, they help you measure your progress. Knowing how far you've come is a terrific inspiration to keep on going. When you can look at your progress at each checkpoint and say, "I'm making it," it's the best kind of motivation.

Ask Yourself Three Questions First

It's a good idea to put your goals on paper. Before you do that, ask yourself these three questions:

1) *Do you have a strong emotional commitment to achieving your goals?* When you have an emotional commitment, your goals are constantly on your mind. You are really into reaching them.

2) *Even though you may badly want to reach them, can you handle in a mature fashion the possibility that you may fall short of full achievement?* A lot of people don't dare to set a goal for fear they can't handle the disappointment if they don't make it.

3) *Are you prepared to invest the proper amount of activity to achieve your goals?* Are you willing to pay the price?

Far better it is to dare mighty things, to win glorious triumphs even though checkered by failure, than to rank with those poor souls who neither enjoy nor suffer much because they live in that gray twilight that knows neither victory nor defeat.

Teddy Roosevelt

Goals Need a Timetable

You can choose a very ambitious goal, such as achieving total financial independence. Or you can seek some modest goal in your family or personal life. A goal is a goal. But one thing all goals need to have in common is that they must be set in time. Someday just won't do. And neither will as soon as I can find some time.

Keep your goals and your progress in front of yourself all the time! A handy record like the one on the next page will accomplish this!

Suppose your goal is to increase your income by $1,000 a month. If each sale you make contributes $100 to your income you will have to make ten more sales each month to achieve your goal. How much sales activity do you need to accomplish this?

Airlines are pretty good at getting from point A to point B. And they generally do it with schedules. So make yourself a schedule. Hour by hour, day by day, plot out how you are going to achieve that goal of ten more sales a month. And remember that any goal can be achieved if you move toward it in small increments, one step at a time. Henry Ford once said "Nothing is particularly difficult if divided into small parts." Divide your time into small parts and make sure each part gets you at least a little closer to your goal. A person who needs to lose fifty pounds can do it in just six months by losing only two pounds a week.

POCKET CALENDAR TABLE

Center	Goal	Results	+ or -
Jan			
Feb			
Mar			
Apr			
May			
Jun			
Jul			
Aug			
Sep			
Oct			
Nov			
Dec			

When the great French philosopher, Voltaire, lay on his deathbed, a visiting friend asked, "If you could have twenty-four more hours to live, how would you spend them?" Voltaire replied: "One at a time."

Hang this in a prominent place above your desk!

WEEKLY GOALS

1 _____	19 _____	37 _____
2 _____	20 _____	38 _____
3 _____	21 _____	39 _____
4 _____	22 _____	40 _____
5 _____	23 _____	41 _____
6 _____	24 _____	42 _____
7 _____	25 _____	43 _____
8 _____	26 _____	44 _____
9 _____	27 _____	45 _____
10 _____	28 _____	46 _____
11 _____	29 _____	47 _____
12 _____	30 _____	48 _____
13 _____	31 _____	49 _____
14 _____	32 _____	50 _____
15 _____	33 _____	51 _____
16 _____	34 _____	52 _____
17 _____	35 _____	53 _____
18 _____	36 _____	54 _____

RECORD OF WEEKLY ACTIVITIES

Week beginning _____

Program for Problems

It is important to remember that my activity program should be adequate to allow me to reach my sales goals in spite of unexpected problems.

Weekly Goals						

Actual Activity

	Attempts to Get in Front of Prospect						
	In Person	Phone	Presen.	Sales	Referral	Earnings	Other
M							
T							
W							
T							
F							
S							
Total							

After each day's activity, I should be proud to **write it down!**

Goals Help You Advance Faster

One of the most successful salespeople I know—she's head of her own company today—confided to me a few things she had learned about goal setting in her career. A fellow beginner had asked her, "Jo, how long are you going to give yourself to become a manager?"

The question stopped Jo in her tracks. She realized that she really hadn't given much thought to goals beyond making or exceeding next week's quota. She had no real goals for her career. That very evening, she sat down with a pencil and a notepad and worked out her career goals for the next several years. It was a real turning point in her life.

Today, Jo says, "Most average people who are willing to work and who have a positive attitude can learn to sell. But your sales career will progress much faster when you start out with specific goals. Goals build your momentum more rapidly. And they help you push obstacles and setbacks out of the way as you go along."

Tie Your Goals to a Specific Amount of Activity

Let's go back to that example of adding $1,000 a month to your income. Most salespeople can translate a goal like that into specifics pretty easily. In some companies, for example, that increased income might come from three sources: personal sales, team sales, and recruiting new reps. You can get out your calculator and figure which combination of all three is most likely to get you the extra $1,000. Then, if team sales are worth 60 percent of your effort, make sure that what you're doing is in line with what you hope to achieve.

Goals Can Help You Keep a Good Attitude

Salespeople with specific goals and a strong commitment to achieving them always seem more positive than those who don't have goals. In a way, a goal is a very effective protection from negative influences. When you have your eye on a goal, you are better able to handle the irritations that are bound to come on a daily basis.

Just the other day, one of my managers, who is doing an exceptional job, told me that the only "down days" she has in her life are those days for which she doesn't set goals.

I plan to talk a lot more about attitude later. For now, let me just quote a very successful salesperson whom I have known for many years: "Goals for me are like the rudder on a ship. They steer me. I haven't sailed aimlessly in this business since I started sitting down and putting my goals in writing."

MONTHLY GOAL SYSTEM

Monthly goal setting depends on a total plan of action that involves a specific amount of activity on a daily basis. The amount of activity will vary according to various factors such as closing average, average commission per sale, etc.

	Minimum Quota	Goal
1. Total income needed		
2. Total sales needed		
3. Average commissions per sale		
4. Law of averages		
5. Total presentations needed		
6. Income per presentation		

Watch for Pitfalls

When you sit down to do your goal-setting homework, watch out for these three pitfalls.

1) *Don't make your goals too rigid and unrealistic.* When Jo's friend asked her how long she expected to take to make the manager's ranks, she might have said, "Oh, five or six months." For a sales beginner in that company, that would have been unrealistic. If Jo had also maintained a rigid attitude toward her unrealistic goal, she would have been on a collision course with her company and its promotion policies. Jo would have been in for a big letdown, and chances are her career would have suffered. As it turned out, Jo didn't make that mistake. Don't you make it, either.

2) *Make your goals challenging.* One company I know used a mailer to recruit new salespeople. The mailer asked, "How much money do you want to make this summer?" and gave respondents the choice of circling $1,000, or $2,000, or $5,000. As many as 70 percent of the respondents circled $1,000. Isn't it interesting that more people indicated the lower amount when the mailing clearly indicated that higher earnings were available?

Don't think too small!

3) *Get started toward your goal now.* If "the road to hell is paved with good intentions," then undoubtedly the paving stones are held together with unfulfilled goals.

Of course, no one really means to leave their goals unmet. At the time they set them up, they fully intend to do everything possible to achieve the whole shebang. But then the procrastination begins. The distractions pile up, and they find out that more work is involved than they realized. And the goal just sits there, neglected, to gather dust.

I have no solution for inaction except action. It comes back, once again, to having a "creative confrontation" with yourself. Pace your goal boldly as a challenge worth accepting. Then get on with it. And *do it now.* Right now.

Don't Kid Yourself

If you reach a monthly goal in ten days, it makes sense to revise your goal upward. Likewise, if you can't seem to reach a monthly goal in three, you may be overreaching.

But don't pull the wool over your own eyes. Level with yourself. It is really the goal that needs adjusting? Or is it your way of going after it?

Plan a Whole Lifetime

Some astute person has said, "Most of us spend more time planning a two-week vacation than we do planning our whole lives. We think we can control what happens in the next two weeks. But a whole lifetime is just too big a task to handle.

But if you can plan two weeks, you can most certainly plan a lifetime in two-week segments. Decide where you want to be five years from now, ten years from now. Then break it down into bite-size chunks you can handle easily.

Remember to Review

Earlier, I pointed out that setting goals helps you check how far you've come and how much farther you have to go. But that can only happen if you review your progress at specific intervals. So, when you sit down to plan your goals, plan *when you'll review them,* too. And tie your periodic reviews to the calendar. No matter what else is happening, review on schedule. It's the best way to avoid getting totally off track.

The Five P's: Prior Planning Prevents Poor Performance

Fix that phrase in your brain forever. I promise you, those are golden words. Memorize them and think about them often. To be specific, here's how I recommend you plan each day:

1) *Write down everything you have to do today.* Put down all the possible sales calls you were thinking of making plus any administrative chores you have to do and anything else you can think of. Do it quickly, before your day starts.

2) *Rank everything in order of importance.* Ask yourself, "is this activity directly related to getting business for me?" Then rank it accordingly.

3) *Get rid of the dead wood.* There will usually be a few items on your list that aren't going to contribute anything to your business. One may be a business activity that you enjoy doing but that doesn't have a high payoff. Get rid of it.

4) *Decide which items are "urgent" and which are simply "important."* Be honest. Don't kid yourself.

It's Called Prioritizing

Do all of the above, and in just a few minutes, you have organized your day. You have maximized your chances of coming home later in the day feeling like a conquering hero.

What you've done is called prioritizing. And it isn't hard to do if you're willing to be honest, courageous, and purposeful.

It actually forces you to do some things you probably would not do otherwise. For example:

— It forces you to cross out activities that deliver comfort and comradeship but no sales.

— It forces you to eliminate activities and calls that may take 75 percent of your time to produce 25 percent of your sales.

— It forces you to do away with nonselling activities—especially "waiting" time, office routine, or needless detail work that may really be masking procrastination.

Prioritizing Gets Rid of "Time-Killers"

Here are the five worst time-killers I've ever run into. If they sound familiar, use prioritizing to help get rid of them.

1) *People who think your time is their time.* Too often, this makes your time worthless. If you are in direct selling, lots of your friends treat you as though you don't have a real job. Make it clear to these people that your time is important. If they can't grasp this, avoid them.

2) *The disease called "telephonitis."* It affects a lot of people today. Cure it by not making unnecessary calls and by limiting the length of all your calls.

3) *One hundred kinds of distractions.* From watching the end of a TV show to spinning your wheels shopping for something you don't need.

4) *Errand running.* You know you'll be passing Tillie's Tailor Shop. So you decide to stop and pick up your shirts. Don't. Do it Saturday.

5) *Not listening.* Which means you may have to backtrack later just to check out what it was that someone told you. Learn to listen, take notes, and check the details.

Rate Your Time

"I picture it this way," one of the highest-producing sales-people I've ever known said to me one day. "I have at least four kinds of working time. And I rank them in order of importance." Here's his list:

1) Time actually spent with a prospect.

2) Time spent doing things to get in front of prospect.

3) Time spent preparing for my sales presentation.

4) Time spent nurturing my relationship with repeat customers.

"All four kinds of time are important," he said. "But number one is the most important of all. And all the others are to help me spend as much time as possible in front of prospects."

Use an Egg-Timer

Earlier, I mentioned *telephonitis* as a disease to avoid. You can avoid succumbing to telephonitis if you keep an egg-timer on your desk. Before you make a call, jot down the things you need to discuss with the person you're calling.

For example:

Call Mary Jones

— Invite to Wednesday meeting

— Mention exciting guest speaker

— Offer ride

— Encourage her to bring a sale or a recruit to meeting.

Then call Mary and, as soon as she answers, turn over your egg-timer and limit your call to the three minutes you'll have until the salt runs to the bottom. You'll rarely need more time than that to do what you need to do.

Avoid "telephonitis" by using an egg-timer on your phone calls.

Charting Your Time

Your local stationery store has a wide selection of desk diaries or daily journals you can use to chart your time day by day. It takes only a few minutes to do it each day. Yet, as time goes by, what you eventually have is a priceless record of what you did each day, what worked and didn't work, and much more. It's time well spent—those few minutes it takes to keep your charting current.

Rating your time and charting your time go hand in hand. If the time you spend in front of prospects is the most important time of all, your records should show you what percentage of your time is spent doing that. It may not be enough. But you may never know unless you keep track.

Recently, one company did a survey that showed low producers spent less than half of the amount of time in front of prospects than the high achievers spent, even though all of them were full-time salespeople. How much of your time do you spend in front of prospects? If you don't know, start keeping records.

On the following pages, I've offered a couple of charts you may want to use in planning and recording your daily and weekly activities. I've suggested the kinds of information I feel is important that you record. You may want to modify these charts to suit your own particular business. Feel free to do so. What's important is that the data you enter on these charts are appropriate for the goals you've set.

I don't expect you to keep this time log on a regular basis. However, using it periodically will show you significant segments of time in your day that can be used more productively.

For fiscal week # _____ *From* _____ *To* _____

Goals		Results	
Pers.	Org.	Pers.	Org.

Monday	Tuesday	Wednesday	Thursday	Friday	Saturday
					Sunday

TIME LOG: RECORD OF DAILY ACTIVITY

For: _____

6:00 a.m. _____	12:15 p.m. _____
6:15 a.m. _____	12:30 p.m. _____
6:30 a.m. _____	12:45 p.m. _____
6:45 a.m. _____	1:00 p.m. _____
7:00 a.m. _____	1:15 p.m. _____
7:15 a.m. _____	1:30 p.m. _____
7:30 a.m. _____	1:45 p.m. _____
7:45 a.m. _____	2:00 p.m. _____
8:00 a.m. _____	2:15 p.m. _____
8:15 a.m. _____	2:30 p.m. _____
8:30 a.m. _____	2:45 p.m. _____
8:45 a.m. _____	3:00 p.m. _____
9:00 a.m. _____	3:15 p.m. _____
9:15 a.m. _____	3:30 p.m. _____
9:30 a.m. _____	3:45 p.m. _____
9:45 a.m. _____	4:00 p.m. _____
10:00 a.m. _____	4:15 p.m. _____
10:15 a.m. _____	4:30 p.m. _____
10:30 a.m. _____	4:45 p.m. _____
10:45 a.m. _____	5:00 p.m. _____
11:00 a.m. _____	5:15 p.m. _____
11:15 a.m. _____	5:30 p.m. _____
11:30 a.m. _____	5:45 p.m. _____
11:45 a.m. _____	6:00 p.m. _____
12:00 p.m. _____	Evening _____

SUMMARY

Prior planning really does prevent poor performance. When everything you do fits into a plan—one designed to achieve specific goals—you always have a better idea of where you are, how far you've come, and where you're going. Here's a handy checklist you can use in your planning:

1) Have specific goals.

2) Allow reasonable flexibility in your goals.

3) Schedule enough activity (presentations, shows, etc.) to reach your goals.

4) Plan and organize your life so that you have adequate time available to do the amount of work you need to do.

5) Review your goals at specific times to see if you are on schedule.

6) Revise your goals when it seems appropriate. ❏

CHAPTER FIVE

You Are
the Message

O kay, it's test time. I want to test you on how you feel about sales as a career. Take a minute or two to check your answers to this little quiz.

1) Sales is one of the highest-paid occupations in the United States.

☐ True   ☐ False

2) In sales, you get paid what you're worth. In salaried jobs, you're paid what the least effective employee at that level is worth.

☐ True   ☐ False

3) As a salesperson, you're more secure in your work because what you do produces profits. Many other jobs produce overhead.

☐ True   ☐ False

Did you check True for each of these statements? If you did, you're 100 percent right. And I want you to remember that. Because these three points should be the bedrock of your conviction about your chosen profession. Your career in selling deserves every ounce of conviction you can muster. And the more conviction you have, the more you will project to your prospects.

Three Kinds of Conviction

Conviction about yourself ... conviction about your product ... conviction about your company. You need them all.

At a recent sales convention, I ran into Natalie, a diminutive older woman with a remarkable record of success. I asked her to tell me her secret.

"I talk to 'em," replied Natalie, "and I make sure they know that what I have to say is *important*. If the husband's attention starts to wander, I poke him in the chest. 'Now listen to me when I talk to you!' I tell him."

Well, I won't recommend that you go around poking people in the chest. You might get a punch in the nose. Natalie's particular style may not work for you at all. She gets away with it, partly because she catches people by surprise and mostly because it demonstrates her conviction. She makes her prospects feel her message really deserves their attention. So they smile at her chest-poking and listen.

Don't Be a Wimp

Nothing kills conviction like being tentative about what you have to say. If you come on apologetically with a pardon-me-I'm-sorry-to-impose approach, you are probably conveying the impression that neither your job nor your product is very important.

I was providing consulting advice to a company that sold magazine advertising. Jack was a guy who had a new territory with lots of prospects. He ought to have been doing great, but he wasn't. We made some calls together to see what was happening.

The first thing I noticed was the way Jack prefaced every statement he made with some phrase such as "We're hoping to do this and that" or "Eventually, we'd like to do so and so." He made it sound as though none of those things stood much chance of ever coming to pass. So I bought Jack a cup of coffee and made the suggestion to him that he drop all the "maybe's" and "we hope to's." I told him to make it clear that the project was practically ready to go.

Jack listened and took my advice. Within a week, his sales had increased dramatically.

Several years ago, a young man was making sales calls on schools in the prairie provinces of Canada. The company he represented had had a high turnover in sales reps, and he was new at working this particular sales territory. When he introduced himself to one particularly crusty old superintendent—who was well aware of the turnover rate—the super remarked in a sarcastic tone, "Oh, so you're the fellow who's going to give it a try *this* year!"

"No," said the young man very directly, "I'm the one who's going to *do it* this year!"

The superintendent was so taken aback that he invited the young man into his office; and within a year the new sales rep had accomplished what a long string of predecessors had failed to do. His conviction make the difference.

Conviction Implies Believability

A good part o the success of almost any product comes from its wide acceptance by purchasers. A product that does not please its users doesn't have a long market life. If you know that your product has a solid reputation, don't be hesitant to say, as a closing "hook," something like this: "Don't take my word for it. Simply ask ten people you know who have bought it if they'd recommend it. (If possible, have a list of satisfied local purchasers on hand.) I'm confident that at least eight—and maybe ten—will recommend that you buy."

Most won't ask ten, but they might ask two or three. And you will have made a powerful point about satisfied customers and third-party endorsements.

When you can make a statement like that, it almost seems as though you are doing your customers a favor by selling them the product. Conviction is the best way to achieve believability.

Be Wholesomely Opportunistic

Calling at the home of a couple who appeared to be excellent prospects, I found that the husband was out. "I'd like to hear about your product," said the wife, "but my husband won't let me invite strangers into the house when he's not here!"

I glanced around. It was a bright, warm day, and I saw a picnic table under a large, shady tree in the backyard. "Fine," I said, "then shall we sit over there at the picnic table?" She agreed, and I got the sale.

Don't Let Your Conviction Run Away with Itself

A long-time resident of a small town in Texas decided to run for sheriff. He canvassed from house to house. Knocking on Mrs. Tompkins' door, he began to explain politely that he needed every vote he could get. But before he could let go of a half-dozen words, Mrs. Tompkins interrupted him in a fury.

"Sam Beekins," she shrieked, "you've been chasin' women, drinkin' the town dry, and avoidin' work for years! And you expect me to vote for a no-good like you? Get off my porch before I set my dogs on you!"

Back in his car, Sam pondered the incident for a moment or two, then wrote, beside Mrs. Tompkins' name, just one word.

"Doubtful."

Be wholesomely opportunistic! She wouldn't let strangers in the house, but she bought at the picnic table.

Conviction is a wonderful thing. But don't ever let it make you lose touch with reality.

Back Your Conviction

Fran was a successful salesperson who suddenly found herself with a new manager. Some of her co-workers chafed at the unexpected management change. Not Fran.

"Give him a chance," she said. "He's got a tough job. Let him get used to it. Maybe we can all learn something from him." Even though her own track record was superior to that of the new manager, Fran simply "bought" the new manager, lock, stock, and barrel, and began looking for his strong points. She adopted some of his techniques for herself and found them valuable.

Perhaps most important, Fran projected her loyalty to her co-workers. And her enthusiasm was infectious. Largely because of Fran's positive attitude from the beginning, the new sales manager settled in nicely and was a help to the entire sales team. Everyone won.

Build Your Own Enthusiasm

The easiest way I know to start is by asking yourself these four questions:

1) These *are* quality products, aren't they?

2) People do *need* them—and are presently buying them—right?

3) The company's compensation plan offers me substantial *rewards* for the results I produce, doesn't it?

4) The company has a proven *system* that's getting results for others and that I can use, too, doesn't it?

By the time you've answered "Yes!" to all four questions, your enthusiasm should have perked up considerably. Try it.

How to Stay Enthusiastic

Part of my reason for writing this book is to help you to increase your enthusiasm. Today there is a wealth of material in books and on cassettes that you can use. Take advantage of it. And one more thing . . .

Cultivate "Rainy-Day People"

A friend came to visit me in Chicago. We played tennis at my club, showered, then went to dress. Opening his locker, my friend found that the cash in his wallet had been stolen.

He looked a little crestfallen at first, but as we drove home, he said, "You know, it's a darn good thing they only took the cash. I have about six credit cards in there they didn't even touch." A mile later, he said, "You know, I normally carry a couple of hundred bucks around. It's a lucky break that I only had $50 in my wallet." Then, as we were pulling into the driveway, he turned to me excitedly. "Hey," he said, "I just thought of something. This is a business trip. Any expense I incur is tax-deductible. I'm sure my accountant will let me write off that $50 as a business loss!"

In the three miles between the tennis club and my home, my friend managed to convince both of us that having his money stolen from his wallet was the best thing that ever happened to him!

My friend is a very good example of a "rainy-day person." He's a positive thinker, and whenever I need a boost, he's usually one of the first people I think of calling. You probably know some "rainy-day people," too. Cultivate them. Their friendship is priceless. Here's another example . . .

I know a Cajun lady who began selling reference books for the first time when she was in her mid-fifties. A superb salesperson and a good manager, she also did an exceptional job of raising five fine children: a homemaker, an Air Force colonel, a priest, a banker, and a doctor. The doctor struck oil on some land he owned and became extremely wealthy overnight. He went to his mother and said, "Mom, you're 66. You don't have to go around selling books anymore. I have all the money anyone could ever want. Quit this business and take it easy."

The Cajun lady turned to her son and said, "Boy, this business gives me something all your money can't buy. And I intend to keep on doing it!"

Her enthusiasm for what she did made it more important for her to keep going than to take an easy retirement at her son's expense.

Don't Be a Message of Bad News

You *are* the message. But don't let it work against you. It happened to me once. My customer had been buying my product on a monthly installment plan. The company at that time offered customers this financing with no interest or service charge added. I thought this was a great benefit for my customers and I told them so. Then the company changed the policy and introduced a service charge of one-half of one percent per month. In dollars and cents, it didn't amount to much extra for the prospect to pay each month. But it bothered me to have to tell them about it.

On the first day after I heard about the service charge, I made two sales. Within a couple of days, both had been canceled. Both customers said they had thought it over and would rather wait until they could pay cash to avoid the service charge. I thought about it and realized I was the problem. I'd let this small change bother me so much I was flashing negative messages at the prospects without fully realizing it.

I forced myself to clear my head and concentrate on how inconsequential this service charge really was. Soon, things were back to normal.

The point is that it's really the *inner you* that's the message. And it's what goes on inside your head that counts most of all. Just the same, the *external you is* what expresses that message, and it's important to pay attention to the way you *talk,* the way you *look,* and the way you *act.*

The Way You Talk

The way you talk is as personal as your fingerprint. As long as you have an acceptable level of skill in the use of words—and a reasonably pleasant delivery—you'll most likely do just fine. Don't worry about personal idiosyncrasies such as a regional or foreign accent. Many prospects may find such an accent "charming."

Telling corny or off-color jokes may offend some and invite rejection. Tell the truth, listen carefully, and don't argue or criticize. And remember that eye contact with your prospect as you speak shows confidence and establishes rapport.

Finally, know when to *stop* talking.

The Way You Look

All of us have personal preferences in dress. A good salesperson, however, should probably save his or her favorite sweater and jeans for weekend lounging around the house. On the job, clothes should fit the norms of good business dress. I recommend you read Malloy's *Dress for Success.* You may find it a little more conservative than you'd like, but it's a good place to begin.

Top salesperson Kay McGinnis says, "I need to feel good, outside and inside, so that I feel both prepared for the selling process and happy to be going about it."

The Way You Act

Walk in, look your prospect in the eye, shake hands firmly. Sit down. Reach into your briefcase. Spread out the sales materials. Fold papers. Make a note. All these actions express your inner message in some way—whether you want them to or not. Some call it "body language." Be aware of it and remember that what it *should* be communicating is enthusiasm and conviction.

Manners send another kind of message. Remember that manners boil down to expressing courtesy and showing consideration for the feelings of others. *Care* about your prospect's feelings and it will show.

I'm ending this chapter with a checklist of do's and don'ts that may help you put together the kind of message you intend to deliver.

A Checklist of Do's and Don'ts

Jog your memory. Run through the following list and classify each as a "Do" or a "Don't." Each item touches on some aspect of the externals that project what you are and that make you the message.

	<u>Do</u>	<u>Don't</u>
1. Break in when others are talking	___	___
2. Smile continually	___	___
3. Discourage questions	___	___
4. Tell the truth always	___	___
5. Chew gum while with a prospect	___	___
6. Give flip answers	___	___
7. Practice eye-to-eye contact	___	___
8. Listen when another talks	___	___
9. Wear topsider shoes without socks	___	___
10. Brag about the kids	___	___
11. List personal preferences in food	___	___
12. Have an irritating laugh	___	___
13. Talk incessantly	___	___
14. Spread rumors	___	___
15. Break a confidence	___	___
16. Criticize by name	___	___
17. Arrive late	___	___
18. Use first names	___	___
19. Crack off-color jokes	___	___
20. Ask personal questions	___	___
21. Overstay normal welcome	___	___
22. Lose my temper	___	___
23. Need a shampoo	___	___

SUMMARY

You are the message. You can make that message a compelling one through conviction and enthusiasm. And you can express it most powerfully through careful attention to the way you talk, the way you look, and the way you act. ❏

CHAPTER SIX

Finding Prospects and the LIBK Rule

here are seven steps to successful selling, and I'd like to start by arranging them in pyramid form. Here they are:

Get More Prospects

Sealing the Sale

Closing

The Sales Interview

Build Rapport, Qualify

Get in Front of the Prospect

Get a Prospect

Prospecting helps turn the dream of success into the reality of money in the bank. I've carefully observed some of the world's best salespeople over the past twenty-five years. Some had great personalities. They all had different physical attributes. But they had one thing in common: They all knew how to find a prospect and how to get in front of that prospect.

ALWAYS HAVE A GOOD PROSPECT LINED UP

In my opinion, it's the first rule of selling. To dramatize it, I've said the following in speeches before sales groups as far apart as Lubbock, Texas, and Sydney, Australia:

> "Ladies and gentlemen, on my way here from the airport, I told my cab driver that I was coming to talk to you today. 'That's a coincidence,' he said, 'I was just telling my wife last night that I thought we should buy your product. Is there anyone I could call about it?' Well, I took down his name and phone number, and I was wondering if there's anyone here today who'd like to give the man a call."

At this point a forest of hands goes up. Then I'd say:

> "Sorry, folks. I was just trying to make a point. I'll bet at least some of you here today haven't made any calls this week. But with a chance to call on a qualified prospect who'll be receptive to your presentation, you can hardly wait to get going! I made up the cabdriver story to dramatize the importance of always having a good prospect lined up!"

Top producers always know it; everyone—yes, everyone—could be a prospective customer. Young, old, rich, poor, fat, thin, whatever. Granted, some are more *likely* to buy than others. But assume they're *all* prospects going in—then rate them according to their likelihood.

A TALE OF TWO STOCKBROKERS

Here's a real-life example of two actual sales-people. Broker B is with a firm that strongly emphasizes grassroots prospecting. The other is with a firm that spends a full year training sales people on "the product"—but is very weak on teaching creative selling, especially prospecting.

	Broker A	Broker B
Age	48	24
Sales experience	15 yrs.	none
Local influence	lots	new to area
Training in brokerage business	full yr. with salary	limited; on the job
Commissions earned first year on the job	$22,000	$50,000

A recent study shows 60 percent of salespeople fail to ask for a referral at the end of a demonstration. I have to confess that makes me shudder. It means six out of ten are overlooking the most basic of all prospecting techniques.

Does it pay to go after clients? To be a resourceful prospector? The comparison above is proof that it does. Imagine a man in his early twenties earning more than *twice* as much as an older, more experienced man in the same business! Yes, I'm sure that the forty-eight-year-old man must accept some blame for not motivating himself. The fact remains that a younger man with a more creative approach did outperform a man with far more experience.

Prospects Are Everywhere

Where do you start looking for prospects? At home. In the house next door. In the apartment across the street.

When do you stop looking? At the point where the cost in time exceeds the possible gain.

A professional salesperson I know regularly questions her children about their friends. She gets a lot of information about those friends, their parents, their lifestyles. She is personally interested, but she is also measuring, scrutinizing, looking for prospects. Using that technique, she has increased her business tremendously.

From People to Prospects

In discussing prospecting, the art of finding potential customers, we are not talking about direct mail or direct marketing or classified or display ads. Those methods have worked for thousands of companies. Some firms have used them to produce sales leads for selling face-to-face.

More explicitly, we are dissecting a process in which the face-to-face salesperson remains always aware that every individual may be a prospect. As a salesperson, you can school yourself to think of everyone in this way. People become prospects. You do not disregard their essential humanity; you merely accept the fact that each may represent a future sale.

Also, to your advantage, you start to see a group of people as made up of individuals. You can visualize each as a human entity with distinctive tastes, preferences, personality, and needs. In the group, there may be a bank teller, a truck driver, a champion racquetball player, a beautician, a teacher—and a *prospect*.

The Basic Technique

Like everything else in face-to-face selling, prospecting requires good technique. As always, technique makes your work more effective.

Descriptions of some proven techniques follow. If they spur some creative thinking, some exploration of still other methods, so much the better. *You can develop skill in the use of existing techniques, new techniques, and your own variations.*

The key prospecting methods can be examined under seven headings.

Cold Calls The cold call is just that. You knock on a door or ring a bell and find yourself addressing a stranger who did not expect you.

Many face-to-face sellers avoid the cold-call approach as they would a nuclear waste dump. Others do very well using this method. If it's your bag, you can make it work for you. The essential qualities of dedication, fortitude, and perseverance come into play here just as in other methods of prospecting and selling.

Personal Sphere of Influence How many people do you know? How many are nodding, waving, good-morning-greeting, and chit-chatting acquaintances? How many are honest-to-goodness friends? How many are in your neighborhood association? Racquetball opponents? Fellow church-goers?

Think of this: In his book, *How to Sell Anyone Anything*, champion car salesman Joe Girard states that the average person you meet has a sphere of influence that includes about 250 people who will provide a favorable audience for your product or service—in short, 250 prospects.

If you think about it, you probably have some kind of special relationship with more than 250 people. You may have the beginnings of a great selling career in that group alone. Each of those people has at least 250 friends or acquaintances who might also be excellent prospects.

Why not start asking?

Standard Referral This subject has come up before. Most salespersons regard it as the closest approximation to the ideal prospecting technique.

It involves this: After making a presentation, whether a sale has resulted or not, the salesperson obtains the name or names of others who may be interested in knowing about the product or service.

Used correctly, a referral will become a self-perpetuating source of prospects for you—on an ongoing basis.

Existing Customers   Current or former customers, especially *satisfied* customers, can be prolific sources of prospects. Many will help you out of a sense of appreciation or a feeling of belonging to the same club—your club.

My advice: Never neglect those people you've already sold. On the contrary, let them know how much you appreciate their business. Send each of them a thank-you note. Exceptional salespeople frequently develop mailing lists of clients and mail them periodic updates on their product or service and inform them of changes in the field. If, on the other hand, you do neglect the people you sell to, you run the risk of bumping into those former customers and hearing that they just bought from someone else.

I've started many a great selling day by taking a few minutes to call on an old customer. I usually get a lead or two, and they always make me feel good about my product.

Nest System   You find Prospect Mary through a referral from a friend of hers. It turns out she's a nurse on a very close-knit staff. Mary refers you to a dozen other nurses. You have located a "nest."

Prospects in a nest may work, play, associate informally, or pray together. They may number in the dozens. For you, the nest can represent a rich lode of prospects to be mined. One dentist can refer you to ten or twenty others who may be prospects. A man or woman working in a department in a manufacturing plant may be able to do the same.

Most people belong to a nest of one kind or another. Why not make prospects of the members?

Centers of Influence Centers of influence differ from nests in one key respect: They consist of groups, large or small, that you learn about through an important person.

Examples? A plant manager refers you to his entire staff of foremen. The president of a professional group gives you the names of all twenty-two members. A minister lists some of the more important members of his congregation.

Influence can also derive from wealth. A civic leader may have immense influence. So may a person who has won fame for some accomplishment.

The principle is simple. In following up on leads from a person of influence, you are going armed, in effect, with a recommendation from someone the prospect respects.

Nest prospecting—a key way to find sales

The Buddy System   This happened to me: Early in my career, I decided to try working with a close friend, a former teacher and high school coach, who lacked selling confidence but "knew everybody in town."

Wherever we went, someone would say, "Hi, Coach Mack!" Selling became easy. Coach Mack found the prospects; I made the presentation. All Coach Mack had to do was sit there and say, "They are great products." The combination of our contacts and talents produced a fabulous summer.

The buddy system has worked well under diverse circumstances and in widely scattered communities. In one case, the professional salesperson's buddy had won local fame as a law-enforcement officer. In another, the buddy had led a successful fight for civic reform. A third had gained fame on the basketball court.

Vary Your Basic Techniques

I've already mentioned some variations on these basic methods. They exist in quantity. Every top face-to-face producer I've known had some unique twists.

All were in good taste. All highlight sales results.

Just for starters . . .

For starters, think of the following possibilities. I have used them all at one time or another.

- Calling on a prospect and finding no one at home, you leave a door hanger on the knob. It reads: "Sorry I missed you. This is what my product or service does . . . This is what's in it for you . . . Call me at this number."

- In a similar situation, you leave some materials for the customer to peruse. "Thought about another purchase?" the note on the materials reads. "Can I stop by Saturday?"

- To obtain a referral, promise a reward. A thoughtful, ingenious salesperson working for a pay TV service used this technique repeatedly. Faced once with a prospect who resisted buying because of the installation charge, the salesperson offered free installation if two of her friends purchased the service.

  The prospect went to the phone and started calling her friends and neighbors. Within twenty minutes she had four new prospects who were already half sold. Within two hours, three of them bought. The salesperson now had four happy customers, including the initial "can't afford" prospect.

Hello! Sorry I missed you today. As your local representative, I can save you money and get you installed this week with a no-risk trial offer. You sign no contract. Invite me to drop by, and in ten minutes I'll explain the details. Absolutely no obligation. Call me today.

Phone _____ **or**

_____

How many variations can you devise? Remember, the field in which you work will undoubtedly influence your choices.

Some Refinements

At least four of the prospecting techniques that I've noted involved referrals. The four are the Standard Referral, the Existing Customer, the Nest System, and the Centers of Influence methods.

You can obviously approach prospecting through any of the referral methods on a long-term basis. Properly nurtured, a center of influence can supply you with the names of good prospects for months or years to come. The same might be said of the next contact.

Just as obviously, you need both skill and determination to ask for referrals. You don't want to appear to be asking for too much. You fear a negative reaction. You have another call to make, and are in a hurry.

Forget the distractions. Get referrals. Refine your technique through application of some or all of the following methods.

Have a prospecting goal—or goals. Know how many centers of influence you want to develop in a given period— and find them!

Improve your memory. Few things impress a prospect or client more than quick, easy recall of the name of someone of local prominence who bought your product or service (see Chapter 11, "Group Selling"). Memory will serve you in dozens of other ways.

Get lots of information. Accumulate as much as possible. The prospect's job, family status, interests—they can all be important. Thousands of salespeople make calls after taking a name off a mailbox—or something else. This works, but it has its limitations. In one incident that took place when I was doing cold-call selling in rural Canada, when I was new in the area, I saw a milk can with the letters NADP on it. I went to the door and when it opened, said, "Mrs. NADP?"

"NADP" Oh. NADP stands for Northern Alberta Dairy Products."

Record referrals and leads systematically. A 3" x 5" card file served me well for years. Others have used other systems. If you have a computer, your task will be even easier. But all skilled salespeople keeping such records write down everything they can learn about the prospect. If the customer hesitates over a name, ask her to give it to you even if it looks like a cold lead. Then, with the customer's help, try to rate the prospect.

Rate your prospects. Remember that you'll want to rate all the prospects in your file. The rating notation belongs on the prospect's record.

Get to the new prospects while they're hot! If you receive a likely looking name on Tuesday, you should be following up on the same Tuesday, if possible. Your enthusiasm for that particular prospect will be at its peak immediately after you receive the referral. By Thursday you will be less excited, and in two weeks it may be stale. Use your desk calendar as a tickler if no other system works. You have to use common sense, of course, to get to the prospect at the right time.

The LIBK Rule

Can you pronounce LIBK? It stands for Let It Be Known. It means that you can't hide your selling light under a bushel if you're going to make it in this challenging field.

Let it be known that you're in face-to-face selling—and in what part of it. Whether you are enthusiastically selling Fuller Brushes, houses, Mary Kay Cosmetics, cookware, paintings, or computers, prospects are everywhere. Virtually every human contact you make offers you an opportunity to Let It Be Known what business you're in.

You can't hide your light under a bushel basket. People need to know you're in business!

That applies when you're traveling on an airplane, attending a wedding reception, or chatting with someone in the line at the supermarket.

How do most people work it into their conversations? They ask, "What do you do?" If you show that you're proud of your work and can make a good impression as a person, you will often find yourself talking with a brand-new prospect—one you didn't know you were going to get.

You can be selling all the time, even when you're not actually working. Selling yourself, observing, making notes— they all contribute to your success.

Don't Overlook the Obvious

Prospecting clearly calls for application of one of Sherlock Holmes' principles: Don't overlook the obvious.

While I was trying to sell some real estate through a brokerage firm, the validity of this principle was forcefully brought home to me. The real estate, a farm, had been on the market for two years. Nothing had happened. After several listings had expired, I decided to take a shot at selling it myself.

I had subdivided the farm into seven parcels. The first thing I did was call on the half-dozen or so property owners whose land abutted on mine. I called them from Chicago, then visited them at their homes in Pennsylvania. Within three days, I had sold pieces of the property to four of these individuals.

I'm not knocking real estate people. Many of them are highly skilled salespersons. But the firm that had my listing had its eyes focused on potential out-of-town buyers. This was not surprising, because most of the local farmland was being sold to out-of-town people. But they had overlooked the obvious—that many landowners may be interested in purchasing property adjacent to or near their own.

Tools and Ratings

Now think tools. What others—besides your desk calendar and prospect file—will help you?

Your company can undoubtedly help. Does it supply lists. Door hangers? Referral gifts? Company brochures? Anything that will simplify the task of finding prospects?

Are you using your car and your road maps to the best advantage? The car can get you to home shows, parties, or sales calls and thus to prospects—or it can trap you. Long trips can give you the feeling that you're working when you're not. Maps and good directions save you time.

Creative prospecting methods are everywhere. One office furniture salesman took photos at construction sites, then presented the pictures of the partially finished building to the construction supervisor. The supervisor was thrilled to have the pictures, a memento of his project. The salesman then asked for and quickly received the name and phone number of the person who would be responsible for furnishing the building.

That afternoon he made an appointment to see the buyer.

Ratings? Why not use the A, B, and C categories? "A" represents an excellent prospect. "B" indicates a good quality prospect. "C" identifies a mediocre one.

Some successful salespeople use a four-part rating system. Or a five-part one. Use the system you're most comfortable with.

SERVICE WHAT YOU SELL

Do you know how many people out there are thoroughly disgusted with the poor service—or lack of service—they receive? Some of them wear out their telephones trying to get help.

Do you know how good you'll look if you take the trouble to show you care about your customers after they have bought?

Not all salespeople neglect their customers, but many do. And I'm not suggesting that you follow through with service just to prove how noble you are. But follow-through pays off in a variety of ways.

Make a service call on a customer soon after closing the sale. Make sure the customer understands the product or service and is getting the maximum benefit from it. Answer any questions that may surface.

Then prospect. Obtain repeat business, present and future. Ask for prospects' names that may have been forgotten or overlooked earlier.

Do it quickly. The customer is usually most enthusiastic right after the sale and delivery. Cash in on this enthusiasm.

How to Use a Prospecting Card

How to Ask for a Referral After your demonstration, say to the customer:

"I want to leave my name and phone number in a place where your keep you best friends' names and numbers—under the letters XYZ for the initials of our widget company," for example.

"Mrs. Customer, my job is to explain our product to three interested people a day. Who among your friends and acquaintances would benefit from learning about this product?" (Reach for the prospecting card and write down the referral's name.) "Thank you! Who else? Mrs. Customer, can you think of one more? Thank you! You are very helpful.

"If you were in my place, which of these persons would you call on first?"

"If your friends were sitting here in your dining room, I'm sure you would introduce them to me. Your friends don't know me, but they are entitled to know what is available for their (family, home, etc.), so we offer this introduction card. My name goes here . . .Yours goes here . . .Thank you." (Now fill out the rest of the prospecting card.)

Your goal should be to average at least two new referrals per presentation, whether you sell or not, with at least one signed introduction.

Door Approach with a Signed Introduction Card
"Hi! Are you Mrs. _____ ? I'm _____ .
I'm so glad you're home! I was visiting your friend Mary, giving her a presentation of our (product), and she suggested

that I stop by and see you while I was in the area. This should take about twelve minutes. May I step in?"

"What's it about?"

"It's about (product). Here's a note (fold and tear off the signed introduction card) concerning my visit. Is there a place where we can sit and talk for twelve minutes? Thank you."

Twelve minutes should cover rapport building, qualifying, and part of the presentation, including need building and introduction of your product.

Hints for Successful Prospecting

1) *Sell those who sell you:*
   - Insurance (life/home/health/car)
   - Dry cleaners
   - Grocers
   - Banking services
   - Clothing
   - Cosmetics
   - Legal services
   - Dental care
   - Tennis/Golf lessons
   - Auto/Gas/Tires/Repairs

2) *Look for prospects on your holiday card address list*

3) *Review your high school yearbook*

4) *Sell business associates and former associates*

5) *Call on owners of your product or service*

6) *Talk to friends where you worship*

7) *Contact parents of children's friends*

8) *Check out P.TA./Garden Club/Little League or other groups with whom you have involvement*

Your list of categories of prospects may be much longer than this. Even your best category may not appear. This subject deserves your best thinking.

SUMMARY

As we pointed out in a previous chapter, when you're not in front of a prospect, you're unemployed. If you expect to succeed in selling, you have to learn to prospect. Prospecting skills can make the difference between success and failure. Prospects are found everywhere—cold calls, your personal circle of influence, in various types of referrals. The quality of prospects will differ, depending on a variety of factors. You need to rate your prospects and call on the best ones first. Prospecting is an ongoing process. Give prospecting the emphasis it deserves, follow the steps just discussed, and you will always have a prospect to call on. ❑

CHAPTER SEVEN

Getting in Front of
the Prospect and
Building Rapport

A reminder—the Seven Steps of Successful Selling:

Get More Prospects

Sealing the Sale

Closing

The Sales Interview

Build Rapport, Qualify

Get in Front of the Prospect

Get a Prospect

You've got a prospect. Or a list of prospects. The second step up in the pyramid is to get in front of them and sell something. That's your purpose—in a nutshell.

Here we'll be emphasizing one-on-one selling. We'll also be talking mainly about big-ticket selling. But everything will be useful in some way to everyone in sales. By studying the techniques I'm going to describe, you can make a dramatic increase in your selling power.

I'm not ruling out your making changes or adaptations. Everyone selling face-to-face has to make adjustments and work out a face-to-face technique—or a telephone technique—that's really comfortable. Even in the same company, no two people will go through a presentation in exactly the same way. Your approach needs to fit *you*.

The key to "getting in front of the prospect" is the way you got the referral—and what you learned about the person. Do you know about the prospect's personal situation, job, family status, and so on? Do you know the best time to visit? Is the prospect on shifts—a factory worker, perhaps, or a police officer?

The kind of information you need and should get when taking a referral depends on your product and the kind of sales effort you are making. You should know in advance what information will be most useful.

With people in business, you can sometimes offer—by phone—to visit early in the morning. Many salespeople have used this approach very successfully. A number of business people have thanked me for visiting as early as 7 a.m. "You know what a hassle we have here during the day," they tell me.

When making the approach to the prospect, you will want to control the conditions as much as possible. They needn't be ideal. But whether you have a ten-, or twenty-, or forty-minute presentation, you'll want the time for the presentation to be without interruption if possible.

Many face-to-face reps use the telephone. Once again, the basic rules apply. You have to project a pleasant personality. You'll want to try to control the conditions if you're arranging an interview. You'll want to study this chapter carefully.

THE SEVEN STEPS

This chapter and the two that follow make up the core, the guts, of this book. These three chapters take you inside the face-to-face selling process in three stages:

Chapter 7   Getting in Front of the Prospect and Building Rapport

Chapter 8   The Sales Presentation

Chapter 9   Getting the Order

Those are the three chapter headings. Also, in these three chapters I'll be giving you a basic seven-step process, a tried-and-proven formula for success in selling. We have already talked about one of those steps—prospecting. The other six steps in the three chapters are these:

Step 2:   Getting in front of the prospect—included in chapter 7.

Step 3:   Building rapport and qualifying the prospect—also covered in chapter 7.

Step 4:   Showing the product or service—discussed in chapter 8.

Step 5:   The closing process—included in chapter 9.

Step 6:   Sealing the sale—covered in chapter 9.

Step 7:   Getting more prospects discussed in chapter 9.

Understanding the Steps of the Sale

Do you have to be aware of each step as you go through it? Not really. You have to be comfortable with what you're doing; you don't want to get too mechanical. But with experience I'm sure you'll find yourself realizing that you're on a particular step of the process and that it may be time to move to the next one.

That has happened to me. Each demonstration seemed to flow more easily as I worked into my own system. The same will happen to you.

I have to stress again that a lot will depend on the kind of product or service you're selling. The company you're working for will probably give you some carefully prepared guidance on what to do and what not to do. Or it may leave you entirely on your own.

Either way you're going to find that all selling has elements in common. The techniques we're sharing here will be important to you in some way.

A Chapter 7 Thought

Character has been defined as the ability to carry out a resolution long after you're out of the mood.

—Author Unknown

You're Unemployed If . . .

Salespeople who are serious about their work know one thing for sure. As a lot of direct sales companies tell their reps, "You're unemployed when you're not in front of a prospect!"

I agree totally with that philosophy. I've used it myself. So get out your prospect cards. Ask yourself, "From whom did I get this referral? Can I use the name of that person?" Everything may be important.

GETTING IN FRONT

Some veteran salespeople say that you could walk up to a house, ring the doorbell, and say, "Good morning, Mrs. Johnson. There's an alligator out in the street. May I step in?"—*if* you have a smile on your face. And of course, as we have pointed out, a pleasant manner is essential. It's especially important in that first minute or so when you're trying to get inside the door.

Watch an experienced person do it. He walks up to the door, sets down his briefcase or kit or whatever, then rings the bell. When the door opens, he says, "Good evening, Mr. Doe, I'm Jim Morris, may I step in?"

I could be the salesperson in this scenario. The method has opened thousands of doors for me. I've set down my briefcase so that I don't look too formal or official. The prospect's eye wouldn't necessarily travel down to see the briefcase. I've kept the greeting as direct as possible.

Other salespeople have techniques that differ slightly from mine. I know one superb direct seller who prefers to say at the outset, "I'm wondering if you'd have a few minutes?" Some salespeople shuffle their feet on the doormat, as if cleaning them. That indicates that you're ready to enter and don't want to mess up the carpeting.

The really important thing is that you feel good inside and show it. Show that you feel good about your work. You may have heard it put this way: You don't need a checkup from the neck up.

Don't Try to Sell It on the Doorstep

You may, and very likely will, get a question from the prospect right away. The prospect might ask 1) "What's it about?" or 2) "Are you selling something?"

Answer to No. 1: "I have a few ideas I'd like to share with you." Or: "I'm in the _____ field and would like to share some ideas with you." Or: "I was talking to Dorothy Jones and she suggested that I stop by."

Answer to No. 2 (said with a smile): "Do I look like a salesperson?"

The cardinal rule: unless your product absolutely dictates it, don't sell on the doorstep. That means you don't say, "I want to *demonstrate* something to you."

Ammunition in Reserve

You'll also want to have some ammunition in reserve—answers to other possible questions. You don't want to get hung up on this doorstep.

One question a *World Book* rep was frequently asked at the door was, "Is it books?" My suggested answer to that was this: "It's more important than just books. . ."

With experience you'll learn to anticipate most of the possible questions. You'll develop your own answers that will open that door wider and get you inside. You'll work out statements like this that anticipate the "no time" excuse: "Hi, I'm calling on busy people. May I . . . ?"

Believability: The Magic Ingredient

From your very first word, you're trying to establish believability. You can't and don't want to say too much. You do want to listen. Even while talking your way in, you want to listen. As Christopher Morley says, "There's only one rule for being a good talker: Be a good listener."

In a sense you're listening your way in—and making yourself believable at the same time. You're also learning about the prospect. You can gauge the family's economic status, perhaps see evidence of hobbies, check the location of the TV set, note the number of books, and so on.

You're talking just enough.

Keep It Noncommercial

If you are selling, you say you're selling. Then, how can you keep selling noncommercial?

By selecting the right words. Anyone can do this. A lot of people use a statement like this:

"I was talking with Joanne Smith the other day. She saw and liked our *program* and suggested I should meet with you to let you *evaluate* it too. I'm confident that you will find my *visit informative.*"

Notice the noncommercial words *program, evaluate, visit,* and *informative.* They pay the prospect a quiet compliment.

"Shall We Sit Here?"

You may not make it inside the front door. That happens at times to all face-to-face sellers. In such cases I usually say, "Well, I'll call at a more convenient time." Sometimes I leave a packet of information.

If the prospect does invite me inside, the first thing I say is, "Shall we sit here?" My thinking is simple. If the prospect keeps you standing, you're not going to get much of his or her time. But once everyone is seated, it's accepted that something important and worthwhile is going to happen. You have become a "guest." Many basic social courtesies apply to both you and your "host" or "hosts."

BUILDING RAPPORT

Earlier, I mentioned the high school coach with whom I worked one summer. He had what I'd call pre-established rapport with many of the families we visited. The same was true of a school counselor who shared my work at a later date. But the counselor's case proved that, once inside, you have to make it clear that you have come to talk business.

The counselor knew everybody in town. After we had been invited inside, it became a habit to chitchat for a while. It made me very uncomfortable. Finally, before making a call, I said to my "buddy," "Could you open with something like this?"

> "Of course, you know me from school. I want to mention that I'm not here on school business, though. I'm here to talk about something that is quite important. I think it will be of real interest to you."

He agreed. It worked. We were covering our flanks. We did not sneak up on people by whipping out a sales prospect after a twenty-minute visit. Some common sense is required here. Calling on friends, you don't want simply to drop in, visit for an hour, then spring your presentation on them.

How about those thousands of other situations where you don't have pre-established rapport? Here are just a few ways to build it . . .

- *Use the prospect's name.* And pronounce it correctly. In a referral situation, you can usually get the correct pronunciation from the person giving you the referral.

   Many times I've had a prospect tell me enthusiastically that I had pronounced a name correctly. Often the prospect would add, "and few people do."

- *Use first name or last?* Opinion is divided. You certainly have to consider a number of factors before using a first name: age, position, the nature of the referral, and so on. You have to play it by ear. A fact: Using the first name builds rapport more quickly.

- *Comment on your relationship with the person who referred you.* "Your cousin, Bill Heath, and I went to college together"—that kind of thing, if it's true.

- *Pay a sincere compliment or show sincere interest.* A compliment is praise that is deserved. Interest is attention paid to something that calls for it. You don't want to gush about something that doesn't deserve praise. But most people have at least one "conversation piece" you can refer to. People like to talk about such things.

  As far as showing interest goes, the subjects are everywhere. Books, skiing, hobbies. Little Johnny's or Jennifer's progress in school.

  Regarding the last one, I made it a practice to say, "Are you satisfied with Susie's progress?" That would generally bring a thoughtful answer. I never said, "How is Susie doing in school?" That question seemed to hold a challenge.

  In asking, "Are you satisfied . . . ?" you generally get a more honest answer than you would otherwise.

  Warning: Don't get sidetracked for an extended period. Remember the counselor.

- *Talk of mutual friends or concerns.* I'm amazed every day at how small the world is. Frequently the prospect and I have found that we had mutual acquaintances. But I always made sure I left a positive image of our mutual acquaintance.

  It's my belief that you can find a common element that links you and the prospect in nearly all cases. It may be sports, religion, kids, cars—almost anything under the sun. But once you find it, you will start discovering the power of mutuality. Both you and the prospect start feeling more comfortable. You've taken a big step toward a sale.

- *Use humor.* A little humor both relaxes the atmosphere and speeds up rapport building. Humor has to be in good taste at all times, of course.

Qualifying Your Prospect

You've been with the prospect two, four, six minutes? You should qualify your prospect quickly. "Qualify" here means you are finding out whether a sale is at least possible.

An outstanding salesperson once told me, "I have only three presentations in me per day. Therefore, I want to use those presentations on honest-to-goodness prospects."

That's sound thinking.

I've found that three basic questions have to be answered in the qualifying stage:

1. *Does the prospect have an open mind about my product?* A prospect needn't be a "ready buyer"—someone who is looking for a place to buy your product or something like it. In most selling situations, ready buyers aren't plentiful. If they were, there wouldn't be any need for a sales force. The company would be foolish to put out substantial compensation to salespeople.

   I'm delighted when I bump into a ready buyer. But because there are so many buyers who are not ready, I've always given priority to finding out whether the prospect has an open mind.

   Some examples of the closed minds that salespersons have run into occur to me. A cosmetics salesperson found that one prospect had religious convictions prohibiting the use of cosmetics. In other cases, prospects have used the product or service before and found it totally unsatisfactory.

2. *Am I talking to a decision maker?* If you're talking to individuals, not companies, with experience you will develop skill in judging whether or not a prospect is capable of making the purchase alone.

   As discussed in chapter 1, we are living in an age of increasing independence for both spouses. Many wives make their own decisions to buy reference sets, household items, wines—and of course cosmetics. But if the wife is home and the husband away, and if she indicates that she and hubby do the grocery shopping together, you can bet that she probably won't make a buying decision alone and that demonstrating your product to her alone is not a wise use of your time and energy!

3. *Can the prospect afford it?* Clearly the size of the "package" you are selling can be a factor. So can family circumstances at a particular time. Heavy medical bills or a precarious job situation can convince prospects that this is not the time to buy. In such cases, it is possible that they can't.

Asking Good Questions the Right Way

Asking the right questions in the right way can be an important part of effective selling. Good questions are definitely needed in the qualifying process.

Good questions should do several things for you; most important, they should provide information that will tell you whether you're talking to the right person. This information should also help you determine what direction to take in the sales presentation.

Example 1: In selling books, do you stress in questions the pleasure or availability of the books for browsing or the very practical help it can give little Bobby? (The latter.)

Example 2: In selling a home, would you sell the potential for profit at resale or the pleasure it will be to live there? (The latter.)

Another Question Technique In qualifying, you might use another question technique that has worked wonders for people selling financial products...

> "If I could introduce you to a program that has produced a 20 percent compounded return for the past decade, without a single down year, would you be interested?"

Questions and the Word "What"   With good reason, the word *what is* more effective in the sales process than the word *why.* The word *what* doesn't put people on the defensive. It makes for brevity. And best of all, it can give you ammunition for the *how*—how you as the face-to-face salesperson can help them.

Example: "What is the biggest challenge in your current sales operation?"

Answer: "Recruiting.

Salesperson: "Very interesting. I'm really glad I came. I have a program that can do _____ for you." Or: "Great, our training company specializes in developing customized recruiting programs."

Example: "What is the most important thing you look for in shoes?"

Answer: "Fit."

Salesperson: "Great. That's our specialty."

Another big dividend: The prospect has just verbalized a need for your product or service.

It can work for you as it has for me. Take a moment, now, and think of a question of this kind that would relate to the product or service you sell. Write it down. . .

"If I could show you a way . . ._____

_____

_____ , you'd be interested,

wouldn't you?"

Any prospect who doesn't answer YES to a question like this is probably not going to be worth your while. The ones who do answer *YES?*—You've begun to condition them mentally to do something they haven't necessarily thought they were going to do, and you have a leg up on which direction your sales presentation will take!

SUMMARY

After you get the prospect, you need to do what is necessary to lead the prospect into a sales interview. When you are visiting the prospect in his or her home, you have to be prepared with appropriate responses to questions about the purpose of the call. If possible, you should avoid starting your presentation until you have a comfortable setting for it. The careful use of noncommercial words or phrases such as *evaluate, inform,* or *sharing ideas* increase your chances of guiding a prospect into a sales presentation. While it is important to have a lot of sales presentations, it is nonproductive to waste sales presentations on poor prospects. ❏

CHAPTER EIGHT

The Sales Presentation

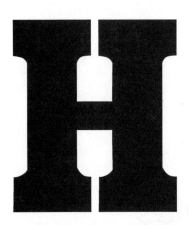

ere's a definition I've always liked: Selling is getting another person to think as you think, feel as you feel, and act as you want him or her to act—in the other person's best interest, of course.

Now consider the sales interview as part of this process. Both sides communicate—with gestures, signals of other kinds, pictures, symbols, words, written materials.

Communication, then, has to be really effective. In selling face-to-face, the two-way aspect may be more important than in any other kind of selling. The face-to-face seller has to listen. Effective selling is not overpowering or trying to wear down the prospect. This may have worked twenty or thirty years ago, but today's prospect is going to be turned off by this approach.

A salesperson using those obsolete methods is going to limit the number of people to whom he or she can sell, will have problems getting referrals, and will have excessive cancellations.

THE INTERVIEW

As a rule, the direct salesperson has to have a prepared presentation. This means that you, the seller, have to know the major points you want to make and the sequence in which you want to make them. But the presentation has to be flexible. Fortunately, each selling situation will be a little different from the previous one. If that were not the case, you would die of boredom.

The face-to-face salesperson has to be ready to respond to these differences. *It's easier to speak convincingly if you know what you want to say.* On the other hand, it's tough to speak forcefully while you're thinking creatively.

None of this means that you are a robot because you have done some preparation. Your routine is not *canned.*

A couple of classic stories show the results of memorizing a completely mechanical presentation. They involve face-to-face sellers who memorized responses for given situations.

Salesperson No. 1: "Will your husband be home soon?"

Wife: "My husband is in the hospital."

Salesperson: "Splendid! Now..."

Salesperson No. 2: "What does your husband do?"

Wife: "He is deceased."

Salesperson: "That must keep him very busy..."

Creating the Need for the Product

The sales interview follows the approach to the prospect. In fact, the interview flows right out of the approach.

Your first challenge when you move into the interview phase is to build *need* or *want* for your product. It is what I call "mentally conditioning" the prospect to be open to buying your product. You may take only a few minutes to do it. But if you do it properly, you greatly increase your chances of getting a sale.

A "canned" sales talk will not do you much good. Listen to your prospect!

In some cases the prospect will reveal a need without any prompting from you. A question may bring out the statement of need, or the prospect may "clue you in" with no hesitation.

Mentally Conditioning Your Prospect

More often, you'll deliberately plant the *"need-seed"* that makes the prospect want your product. The material and method you use may come out of recent news. It may be statistics, facts, projections. The need you build should, in all cases, fit your industry, your product, your service. Sometimes, when calling on a business, you may be aware of the *need* because of public information about the progress or problems of the company.

Many sales companies provide their reps with sales tools that dramatize needs. If you have them, use them.

The frightening facts concerning the reading problems of the American public, revealed by recent governmental studies, give every company selling educational materials for the home a perfect means of establishing need.

Can you think of a way to build need that will fit your situation?

Inadequate, Not Inferior

One of the most expert face-to-face salespersons I've ever met used to say that in building need you were trying to make the prospect feel inadequate, not inferior.

I would describe this basic difference between those two words this way: *inadequate* implies that the prospect has not done everything possible to correct a situation. But you show the prospect that it's not too late to take corrective action (to buy your product or service).

Inferior implies that the prospect is below standard in some way—permanently. The prospect's normal reaction would be anger or defensiveness.

Once again, the process of causing a prospect to feel inadequate depends more on how you say it than on what you say. But you do need relevant facts. You *should* come on politely. You *should* wind up with a question or questions to make it clear that the gravity of the situation is understood.

Obviously, need can flow from basic human motivators. Most of us want status or prestige. We also need acceptance, economic security, recognition, and achievement.

Many professional salespeople see six basic reasons for buying: love, caution, fear, profit, utility, and emulation.

All those things help round out the picture. And give you clues to needs.

Building and Finding Need

You can either *build* need or *find* it! Often, a simple question will bring an answer that uncovers a need.

Questions like these have worked for salespeople in various fields:

"Are you satisfied with...?"

"Are you interested in improving...?"

"Have you a specific concern about...?"

"Have you ever used our product (or service)...?"

"Do you know that cost studies show...?"

"Do you think you have enough...?"

And of course don't forget the best one: "If I can show you a way to..., would you...?"

Painting Vivid Pictures

Need building will be most effective if you can paint vivid pictures. That's true of the entire interview process, in fact.

Working recently with salespeople in training for a pay-TV service, I encouraged them to build need by saying something like this to their prospects:

> "You work hard all day, Mr. Jones. In the evening, you deserve every bit of pleasure you can get out of your leisure hours. You've earned the right to settle back in your favorite armchair with a cold one in your hand and share with your family the pleasure of watching a first-rate movie without a single commercial interruption haven't you?"

I don't remember any prospect saying, "No, I haven't." Over the years, I've made thousands of sales of educational products with the following picture . . .

"Mrs. Smith, as your little Susie goes through her school, will her teachers see a bright, enthusiastic girl with her hand up, ready to answer? Or will they see her with her head bowed, hoping not to be called on?"

Now observe how some experienced salespeople selling financial products work. These face-to-face sellers may encourage prospects to take steps to provide in advance for their youngster's college education.

"Bill and Mary, by setting up a program like this now, you'll have the peace of mind of knowing that the financial part of Susie's education is well taken care of. You'll be able to look forward to enjoying the same pleasure that I saw in the eyes of some proud parents at the (college name) graduation last spring. It's obviously a great feeling to be able to say to yourself, 'Yes, we've done our part in giving Susie the start in life we feel she deserves.' "

Itemize and Summarize

I believe firmly in the power of itemizing and summarizing. You can carry a 3" x 5" card with some key points noted on it and keep it in a handy place. You can refer to it when you need a reminder.

You may itemize several times in a presentation. Why not? It's an effective way of reinforcing significant points.

In need-building, a typical list of points might add up to a summary of the particular situation you are describing.

For example:

> "So you see, Mrs. Jones, what the situation is. I see three things here. One, our schools aren't capable of doing the job they would like to do. Two, that puts an extra burden on the parents. Three, without the kind of help that this program provides at home, a lot of students aren't making the progress they're capable of. It's serious, isn't it?"

A second example:

> "Susie, I think you'd agree that all of us career people need to look our best when we're out in the marketplace. Isn't it true that we have only one chance to make a good first impression? And isn't it true that just the right shade of makeup can really make a difference? Then isn't it also true that the type and quality of the makeup you wear can make a dramatic difference? You know we have an exceptional range of products to help."

The Transition

You've developed the need. The prospect is thinking with you. Now you want to get into the core of your presentation.

You'll work out your own method of making that transition. It can be a few words, a few sentences. I've found this kind of thing very effective:

> By the way, Mr. Martin, regardless of the job you are doing, you need good tools to do a decent job. I was raised in a rural area. I could see that a farmer couldn't do a very good job if he didn't have good equipment. If he had to go back to a mule and a plow, he'd have a tough time feeding the nation—or himself.
>
> "You need equipment. The surgeon wouldn't do a very good job if he had to use Civil War methods. It would be tough to do a heart bypass, wouldn't it?"
>
> "It's the same in the home. The quality of the educational situation at home depends on how good the tools are. That's why I'm here."

Transitions, in short, connect the steps in your presentation.

Showing the Materials

In addition to the product, your company may provide you with a sales talk, brochure, or other sales aids.

Be sure you use them to sell benefits, not features, as much as possible. Don't just show what the product *is* but *what it will do for the prospect.*

Sell What the Prospect Wants to Buy

The real estate agent had a major passion in life. He believed houses should be engineered for efficient operation in all weather.

The potential buyers had told him they were looking for style and living space. The agent talked right past that expression of need. One home the couple looked at seemed to be ideal. But the agent buried them under BTUs, R values, and heat pumps.

Finally, the couple gave up. They left abruptly, leaving the agent scratching his head.

The agent was working from a sheet that gave a hundred details about the house. But he got "hung up" on those details. He forgot to tune in to what the prospects were telling him.

Worse, he sold *features,* not *benefits,* and certainly not style and space.

Using your materials carefully, you may give some parts of the presentation more emphasis than others. You have to use judgment there. You'll find that you're more comfortable with some parts of the sales process and sales tools than with others.

But refer to all the parts at one time or another. If you're using fairly complicated materials and you feel that you get bogged down, or if you find that your demonstration drags at a particular point, you may choose to shorten it.

You want to keep it moving. Keep the prospect interested.

Selling Benefits

Harry Steinberg, a top face-to-face seller, told me once that a price increase in his company's products wouldn't affect him at all.

"I sell benefits, not numbers of pages or illustrations," Harry told me. "They could double the price. It wouldn't affect my sales at all. When you're selling a thousand dollars worth of what it will do for you, what's a 10 or 20 percent price increase?"

You're selling the mouth-watering sizzle.

Take a moment now to jot down the three most important benefits of your product or service.

Benefit No. 1:

Benefit No. 2.

Benefit No. 3.

You may have the most impressive array on earth of cosmetics. Or home beautifiers. Or wines. Or jewelry. But the old sales training adage is still true.

You may think an elephant is a beautiful animal. But that doesn't necessarily mean you want to own one. Just because a product is nice won't sell it. You have to show prospects what it will *do* for *them.*

The Lead Pencil

I'm not saying features are not important. They are. But that importance lies in translating each feature into a specific benefit—something the product will do for the prospect.

Suppose you want to sell a lead pencil. Say the pencil has an eraser on the end. Those are its features.

But what really interests the prospects is how those features translate into *benefits:* You point out that the lead provides a highly versatile way to write or draw, and errors can be corrected quickly by erasing.

Handling Objections

"I ignore objections—politely," says one experienced face-to-face seller.

Another says: "I always have an answer ready. My company has drilled our salespeople on logical responses to objections." This salesperson sells pictures for the home. "There's a natural answer I give *before* someone says, 'I have no wall space.' I just tell everyone in every party group, 'The average house has 42 walls.' That way I anticipate that objection, or forestall it."

---

20 of the Most Common Objections

1) We can't afford it at this time
2) We want to think about it
3) I can't make this decision alone
4) We will buy it next year
5) A relative or friend sells the same product
6) You're coming at a bad time
7) We have plans to spend the money elsewhere
8) The price is too high
9) It's recession time. We're cutting back
10) We have no budget for your product
11) Your company is too big (or small) to handle the order
12) Your service wasn't good last time we bought from you
13) We are satisfied with our present supplier
14) I can't make up my mind
15) You're too late; we've got one already
16) Your product is not the latest style
17) I need to get an expert's opinion on this
18) Your price sounds too low; I'm skeptical
19) We've got one on order
20) Your product hasn't been tested enough

Those answers from two successful face-to-face sellers show that different salespeople have different methods of handling excuses or objections.

Depending on the objection and the way it's stated, my own response is either no response or something like the following that turns the objection into a question:

"Then you really feel that...?" I add some facts that will counter the objection. And I ask more questions. But what I am really trying to find out is whether the prospect means what he or she is saying and to determine whether this is the real reason for hesitation.

In my experience, objections very often have little or no direct connection to facts. They may be excuses. The prospect verbalizes them to take part in the sales negotiations. Or to defend his or her position. The prospect may be trying to slow down or halt the sales process briefly. Possible motives for doing so include the following:

- The prospect has not yet decided to buy.

- The prospect has other questions to ask.

- The prospect wants to let you, the salesperson, know that he or she is still "boss"—that you're not dealing with a pushover.

Remember: A sale is made in every presentation. Either you sell the prospect or the prospect sells you on the fact that it's impossible to buy at this time.

Objections or excuses can be a valuable help to you. They may tell you what's on the prospect's mind. They make face-to-face selling a participative, or two-way, process. You should welcome them.

Emotional Appeals

Regarding the use of emotional appeals, you can find different opinions. Some face-to-face sellers are uncomfortable using emotion and avoid it. Others use emotion very effectively!

Some things to remember about emotional appeals: They have the purpose of leading the prospect toward buying, but if not made carefully and phrased right, they can offend the prospect.

In one case, a salesperson facing the lady of the house was getting nowhere. An emotional appeal involving the man of the house seemed to be called for. The salesperson, looking at a picture of a handsome man on the mantle, asked, "Is that your husband?"

The response was affirmative. The salesperson went on, "He looks like a very nice man. I'm sure he always goes along with your decisions." The answer came back at once.

"He's an S.O.B., and I'm sorry I married him."

The salesperson said, "I guess I misjudged him." The salesperson's technique would have been effective in nine out of ten cases. This just happened to be the tenth.

Common sense is necessary if you use emotion in selling. You'll want to keep in mind that most prospects are more sophisticated than they were a few years ago. You'll want to respect their intelligence.

The emotional appeal may be most appropriate in the "sealing the sale" phase (next chapter). In this phase you are trying to show your prospect-turned-customer that buying was a wise decision.

Making Another Transition

Now you're moving into the "getting the order" part.

The transition many salespeople have found effective runs as follows:

> "By the way, the nicest part about this is that it's so easy to have. (Take out the order pad.) Let me show you how this looks on paper..."

Another method has worked wonders for me. It's actually just two simple points. When I've finished showing the product, I say:

> "I really came here today to accomplish two things, Mr. and Mrs. Johnson. One, I wanted to show you how you can benefit from having this program in your home. Two, if possible, I wanted to work out a way you can have it now."

You may at this point get a question about price. With bigger-ticket items, a lot of salespeople do one of two things:

1. They minimize the figure, saying, "It's only ninety-nine dollars." (They do not say, "It costs nine hundred and ninety-nine dollars.")

2. They do not mention the price at all. They write it on an order pad and show the figure to the prospect, saying, "The good news is that, because of the volume of business we do, you can have it for this small amount."

The salesperson watches for reactions, of course. Both approaches work.

SUMMARY

So the heart of the selling job is the sales interview. Although you don't want a canned sales talk, you do need to be prepared. You need plenty of sales ammunition and a plan for the sequences you will follow in making your important points. Your sales message will be received better and have a greater chance of producing the sale if you prepare your prospect for it by either reminding or showing him or her the *need* he or she has for your product or service.

The need-building process is best accomplished by making prospects feel that they are *inadequate* to do the best job unless they have your product. The sales interview should sell *benefits,* (what the product will do), rather than *features,* (what it is).

Sales prospects frequently voice objections, but the seller should recognize that objections are often only excuses; they don't mean that you won't get a sale. You need to provide leadership for your prospect. Remember, selling is getting people to think the way you want them to think, to feel the way you want them to feel, and act the way you want them to act. ❑

CHAPTER NINE

Getting
the Order

his final phase of the selling process seems to scare some salespeople, especially part-timers. Some find it unnatural. They don't want to seem pushy or overbearing.

If you're feeling a little timid yourself, remind yourself of some facts. *You're not a professional visitor.* You're there on business, and the prospect knows you're there on business. That means that at some point you're going to ask for the order.

Think of this too: About 60 percent of all face-to-face sellers *never ask* for the order, even one time!

The stance you take, the way you talk to people, the way you project—this is what creative confrontation is all about. You know that *how you say it is* more important than *what you say*. We've talked about hundreds of other things. But now we're at what may be the most important part of all.

You've Got To Ask!

Unless you ask for the order, you probably won't make the sale. You've wasted your time.

Remember what they say about Columbus. No one would have blamed him if he had turned back. But no one would have remembered him either. You need to persist.

The Closing Process

Some salespeople like to think of the conclusion or close of a sale as the statement of a few words or a single sentence. That may be accurate where smaller-ticket items are involved. But I believe it's different with bigger-ticket products or services.

Here, it's a process. One that can be plotted step by step. One that anyone can understand and master.

As indicated earlier, the process has three basic parts: the closing process itself, sealing the sale, and getting referrals.

Ask Early and Often

An old sales rule holds that you should "ask (for the order) early and often." The rule is a good one. But how often is often? One authority says four times. Others will tell you five or two.

My answer: It depends on your product or service. The higher the cost, generally, the larger the ticket, the longer your presentation, and the more numerous your chances to ask for the order.

How often you ask may also depend on whether you are using the party plan or the one-on-one method. In party plan selling, orders may rain down on you. Or you will undoubtedly have a point in the program at which you ask for orders.

A kind of group psychology may take hold of those present. It may inhibit order placement or spur it on. Usually it is wise to take the order *first* from the person who has the higher status in the group, providing it appears that person is enthusiastic about your product.

Kinds of Closes

Different authorities classify a "close"—the order-getting phase—in a variety of ways. You can surely find further information on such formats as the following:

The Order-Pad Close You use your order pad as a selling tool. You may, depending on your style and what you're selling, have it in front of you from the moment you sit down. Personally fill out the order.

The Choice-Question Close I have found this one very successful. Again, you would use an order blank. But with it in plain view, you may want to condition the prospect a little more:

> "If you felt this program was something that you were convinced would make a difference, I'm sure you'd be able to afford x dollars a week for it, right?"

The choice-question is appropriate now. To make it easy for the prospect, you'd say this:

> "People pay for it in one of three ways. Some pay cash. Some pay for it over ninety days; others use a monthly payment method.

If you get a positive answer, you would of course keep on writing. "What's the correct address here?" *Never* ask the prospect, "Do you want it or don't you?"

Do you see what's happening? You are giving a something-or-something choice. You are not giving a choice between something and nothing.

Impending Event Close You tie the close to something that may or will happen. The price of the product or service will be higher, for example.

The Additional Value Close In this case, you reinforce the prospect's confidence in making a "buynow" choice. You may repeat a story that makes a good point.

Other types of closes will occur to you. They all share one factor: You are asking for the order. Which one fits you best? You are attempting to "work out a way" for the prospect to benefit from your product.

With some prospects who still seem to be in doubt, you may be able to take stronger action. You reach for a phone and say, "I'm going to see if we can't get delivery in a week." With some prospects, you can practically issue a direct order without offending them in any way.

> "It's very clear that you want this program, I call tell. Go get your checkbook and we'll get the materials on the way to you."

A Chapter 9 Thought

Yesterday is a canceled check; tomorrow is a promissory note; today is ready cash—use it.

—Kay Lyons

The SATMC Method

You encounter an objection. You want to keep moving, but you have to deal with it. The old SATMC method I learned in my initial sales training program may be your best option. The technique works in many different sales situations.

SATMC stands for five words:

Smile

Agree—seem to agree

Turn—turn excuse

More—more value

Close—close differently

The technique is simple. Hearing the objection, you **Smile.** You seem to understand, then you **Agree.** "That's the reaction most people have, frankly." Now you **Turn** the objection into a reason for buying.

> "But you know, you mention that you can't afford it. I was calling on a widow the other day, and she said, 'When I got this product, from a financial standpoint, I had no business buying it. But I really felt at the time that it wasn't an expense, it was an investment. And there hasn't been a day in these past three years that one of the kids hasn't used it. I think it was the best money I ever spent.' "

So the excuse has been turned. But you're not done. You have to present **More** value:

> "By the way, I did neglect to show you one of the most beneficial things about this . . ."

Now you move to **Close** again. But in a different way. You have choices and can invent hundreds of your own:

> "I don't know whether your kids have ever received a package this size in the mail before. We could put their names on the box. Would that be okay, or should we address it directly to you?"

Or:

> "Does a member of your family have a birthday coming up? We could make this a birthday present."

Minimizing Cost

Minimizing the cost of your product or service gives you another way to close. In using this method you are making it easier for the prospect to buy. Here's a common approach:

"You know, cost is pretty much how you look at things. Now, you know your situation and I don't. I'm on the outside looking in. But I do feel—well, I'm not going to twist your arm on this, but what does your grocery bill come to every week?

"Okay, $100. Think with me about this. I'm sure you shop wisely to keep it at that. But what if you got your grocery bill once a year? Say the bill came in today and you had to tell your husband that it's $5,200. That would shake him a bit, right?

"But you don't pay the grocery bill annually. You pay it weekly. Now, can you think of this product in those terms? This program can be owned for just $30 per month or a little more than $7 per week. Would it be a big deal if your grocery bill were $107 and not $100?"

Or:

"I was leafing through a college guide the other day. You could send your Peggy, if she were old enough, to X college for $11,000 a year. That's for nine months.

"At $11,000 a year, you'd be paying more than $1,200 a month. That one month's college cost would be more than the entire price of this product. And the product might make the difference, perhaps provide that additional educational advantage to enable Peggy to go to that particular college."

You've made the cost look minimal. In a sense, of course, it is.

In most cases you can draw your comparisons on the basis of the prospect's income or business. For example, a substitute teacher might earn $100 a day . . .

> "You're talking about one additional subbing day every two months to make the required monthly payment."

You Make the Decision

You keep moving as long as you're getting positive answers—or neutral answers that tell you you're on the right track. But—and this is vital—make the prospect's decisions as much as possible. You decide what the prospect needs.

Many inexperienced salespeople make one deadly mistake when they are showing several or many products. They have their literature out and they ask, "Which ones do you like?"

In deciding for the prospect, you do it differently. Frequently, you can gain the advantage by recommending that the prospect take only *some* of your items, or part of your package ...

> "Some enthusiastic salespeople feel that everyone should have everything. But honestly, your Bobby's in fourth grade. He would benefit from these other books, but—and I'm being very practical—I think you need this one and that one. It'll cost you about half as much."

An advertising space salesperson—or any direct salesperson—could do the same thing, along these lines:

> "I believe, from what you've told me here, that I understand your problem. In view of the message you want to get out, I really do want to suggest that you take a full page. And certainly in order to be able to track the results of the ad, you need to run it a minimum of X number of times."

The Three-Point Close

Still meeting resistance? They want to "think about it"? Try the three-point close. It brings us back to enumeration, or itemization, that wonderfully handy tool. It would go like this, with changes that adapt it to your field:

> "I understand your point of view perfectly. I think you should be discriminating about the buying decisions you make these days. Let me suggest this. Maybe I can think about it with you. I've been counseling families for more than X years, and frankly I've found that the smart, discriminating buyers generally do think about the same things.
>
> "Number one, they ask, 'Is this the product I want?' And I review with them. I ask them—and by the way, let me ask you—is there any question in your mind about the quality of this product? All right, that's one thing you look at.
>
> "Number two, smart buyers ask, 'Is this something that's going to be good for us?' I don't think I need to ask you about that, do I? You seem to feel as your neighbor Mrs._____ did— that it's not an excuse, it's an investment.
>
> "Number three—and I'd be embarrassing you and insulting you if I suggested that you wouldn't answer yes to this. The third thing people ask themselves is 'Can I pay for it?' We have just discussed the three things most discriminating people consider when they 'think about it.'
>
> "Let's go ahead and get the product on the way to you."

"May I Be Candid?"

You have a terrific alternative to the three-pointer. Or, you can use this one *with* the three-pointer. It goes like this:

> "Mr. and Mrs. Allen, could I be very frank with you? Would I insult you if I were totally candid . . . ?"
>
> "All right, I know you have good intentions on that, but I really think that since Bobby has a reading problem you'll probably want to do something about it. It's better to do something now rather than later when you might have to spend a bundle on tutors. Or rather than take the chance that he'd have to live with the stigma of having to repeat a year in school, or do remedial work during the summer vacation."

The fact that you asked their permission to be totally straightforward allows you to be stronger with them without offending them with your candor!

Can you add a point here? Can you stress a service feature that's part of your package? I've found that it can really put a fine touch on your close:

> "You know, you're not just buying a product here. You're getting my expertise with it because I'm as near as your telephone."

Want to keep a "Closing File"? Here's a model form:

	Excuse	Reply	Testi-monial	Transi-tion	Close
Closing File					
Case 1.					
Case 2.					
Case 3.					

Those Vivid Pictures

Paint pictures—again. They can make getting the order so much easier. They may be more important in the order-getting part than in other parts of your presentation.

One that I always liked goes like this:

"I notice you have rubber tires on the tractor out there. You say maybe the kids will go through school without any additional help and that may be. But I know fifty or sixty years ago they didn't have inflatable rubber tires. You could probably still use a tractor without rubber tires but they certainly give you a smoother ride through the fields don't they?"

Now I'll guarantee you that having these materials will give the boys a smoother ride through school."

Got a Sale? Stop!

Mark Twain tells the story of the man listening to a preacher's appeal for money for a particular cause. When the preacher started, the man was impressed. "I think I'll drop $10 on the plate," he thought.

The sermon went on. "Maybe $5 will be enough," the man decided. A while later, with the congregation getting fidgety, the man thought: "This is out of hand. I'm not going to give a cent." In the end, the man took $5 out of the collection plate.

The lesson for the face-to-face salesperson is simple. When you've got a sale, *stop!* You are not so welded to your presentation that you have to run through it from beginning to end after you've made the sale. If you do, the prospect may react like the man in Twain's story. When the prospect is ready to buy, write the order.

Sealing the Sale

Morning dawns. The customer you sold last night has what salespeople call "buyer's remorse."

How bad a case is it? Will the customer call in and cancel? It may depend on how well you sealed the sale.

How Not to Sell a Radio

Author and sales trainer Al Robertson told how he once visited a factory to see a new product line. He learned everything about the product, a radio that could receive programs broadcast from a great distance away. Since he had a store at the time, he ordered some of the radios.

A customer came in, saw the radio, and asked about it. Al told him that the radio contained three miles of wire, had 746 soldered joints, and boasted a preamplifier tube and automatic sound control so that the sound would always remain at the same level. The details poured out.

The prospective customer became restless and nervous. Finally, breaking in during a pause, he said to Al, "Do you have one of these radios that you'd like to sell?"

"Yes, of course." They completed the transaction. As Al rang up the sale, he asked what had motivated the customer to make the purchase.

"Not a thing that you said," came the answer. "In fact, if you hadn't stopped talking, I was going to leave. My brother-in-law told me that this was the only radio that would get Kansas City, and I have a favorite program from there that I want to hear."

Tying the Package

Sealing the sale—or tying the package, as it's been called—means reassuring the customer. A lot of inexperienced salespeople neglect to do it, sometimes because the sale has put them on Cloud Nine.

You are simply trying to make the customer feel good about a buying decision. You can do it a dozen ways. But some that have worked for thousands of face-to-face salespersons are these, spoken perhaps together with a handshake:

> "I want to congratulate you on having done something very important. You've taken a big step toward..."

And:

> "You know, the nice thing about this is, the richest family here in Kenosha, Wisconsin, can't have a better _____ because there isn't a better one."

And a really emotional one...

> "When I see people like you investing in this product it reminds me of the college commencement I attended a couple of springs ago. A young man got up to give his talk and said, 'Ladies and gentlemen, before I start my talk, I want to thank the person who's responsible for my being here today—my mother.' And some people there knew the circumstances. She was a widow with very limited means and had done menial work to put the boy through college. I thought the applause would bring down the rafters when she stood up. I noticed a lot of hankies coming out.
> "You know, this won't solve all of life's problems, but it will certainly take you a long way toward..."
> Believability—again.

Leaving Materials

You can seal the sale in other ways.

If your company makes them available, you can, for example, leave materials on the product or service. While waiting for the product to arrive or the service to start, your customers can be reading about it, learning about it.

If you don't have the materials, you have a reason for coming back. On the return visit, you may be able to prospect some more.

Getting More Prospects

Prospecting was the first of our seven steps. It's also the last. Getting referrals is a form of prospecting.

How many referrals do you try to get out of this last stage of the selling process? As many as possible. But start by asking for two.

You can do it by offering a favor, not asking for one.

The Offered Favor

To me, it's just as simple, and more natural, if you believe in your product or service, to offer a favor. You can do it this way, for example:

"I've really enjoyed visiting with you. It's always pleasant to visit with someone who's as intensely interested in _____ as you are.

"Has my visit been informative for you? You know, I don't have a lot of time, but you've been so nice, I'd like to take the time to call on two people in your circle who might benefit from seeing this (program, product, etc.) Who do you think would be the two most likely persons or families?"

At this point it may be useful to mention that others are buying. The wealthy Van Husens down the street. A well-known pastor. A member of the city council.

If two names are forthcoming, I have primed the pump. But I don't stop. If the customer can provide ten, I'm that much further ahead. It's the endless chain.

Here's a response card one firm uses to get referrals out of seminars:

Has this seminar been informative?

Our goal is to make every seminar we conduct a very worthwhile experience for everyone who attends. We trust that it has been good for you.

You probably can think of several people who would benefit from attending one of our sessions. Would you take a minute and jot down their names? We will see that they get an invitation for a seminar in the near future.

Thank you for your help!

_____

Name   Home Phone   Office Phone

_____

Name   Home Phone   Office Phone

_____

Name   Home Phone   Office Phone

_____

Referred By

Obtaining Information

You need to pay close attention all through this process. Make notes. Ask questions. A few more minutes may provide you with enough referrals to last a week.

You're actually trying to find out all you can about these potential prospects. If they're available, you need names, addresses, telephone numbers, work schedules—all the information we've talked about. You also need permission to mention the source of the referral:

"You don't mind if I use your name, do you?"

Every one of us is tempted to short-cut. We would like to show the product or service or literature and say, "Listen, I've got something to show you." If you've resisted that temptation and made your presentation, you can surely go the last mile.

That means: Get referrals before you leave. Get them whether you made a sale or not.

SUMMARY

Thirty-five Choice Questions or Closing Lines

1. Would you prefer to have delivery on a weekend or a week-day?

2. Would you like to use our monthly payment plan, or would you like to pay cash?

3. I have just one of these discounted models (vacuum cleaner, set of books, etc.) left. Shall I reserve it for you or would you prefer the full-priced one?

4. We can add this additional product onto your order for 30 percent off the regular price. Shall we do this?

5. Would you prefer this in blue or red?

6. This product is a little higher, but I sense that you prefer quality. Would you prefer this one or the standard model?

7. Would you like to have it shipped in the children's names or your names?

8. These are probably the most comfortable shoes made. Would you like these or the ones with the higher fashion look?

9. You're making an exceptional choice—this is a garment of exceptional quality. Shall we fit you for it?

10. Would you like to take it with you today, or shall I ship it to you?

11. We can guarantee this TV set for six months rather than the usual three. Is this important to you?

12. We can guarantee this price for four weeks if you order today. Shall we get it started?

13. This is the last week we can offer it at this amount before the price goes up. May I ship it to you now?

14. Shall we see how this painting looks on your living room wall?

15. This is a limited edition, and we only have a few left. This may be your last chance to have one. Rather than risk not having it available, shall we order it for you today?

16. Would you like us to bill you on the first of the month or on the fifteenth?

17. Would you feel better if we added credit life insurance to your order? Will this give you more peace of mind?

18. Would you like to take advantage of our three-for-the-price-of-two offer?

19. Don't you agree that this is the most attractive product of the entire selection?

20. Is this what you've decided on?

21. If you ever find a problem with the (any feature), just remember our "Quality Guarantee"; we'll replace it!

22. A person like yourself who appreciates quality should have this product. I'll work out a way that you can have it.

23. You save 25 percent by ordering the products as a group. Shall we do it this way?

24. I can hold it until tomorrow if you like—this product is selling quickly and I want you to be able to take advantage of this special offer.

25. Why wait when you can enjoy the program (or other product) today?

26. I'd be insulting you if I suggested you couldn't afford x dollars a month, wouldn't I?

27. You can start with the basic program and order the other products within ninety days at the package price.

28. Would you like me to include the gift page for Bobby and Mary?

29. This product is really a superb investment as well as a good purchase inflation being what it is.

30. If you order today you can have x days to see if you are satisfied.

31. This is the same product that (a celebrity or respected person in the community) uses.

32. You're making a wise decision. This is the best (product) made in this price range.

33. Would you like to take advantage of the cash discount or do you want to use your credit card?

34. For a person whose time is as valuable as yours is I think you can see this is a good investment can't you?

35. Will you be putting it in the living room or the family room? ❑

CHAPTER TEN

Summing Up:
PAT—The Success Formula That Always Works

Presentations + Attitude + Technique. The first letters of each word in this formula spells PAT. It's a simple formula for success in sales that will never fail you. A discussion of this success formula is a natural conclusion for this book's explanation of the total sales process.

A presentation is easy to understand. It's that just discussed, much-ignored process of getting in front of a prospect and giving your sales talk. In party-plan selling it involves getting in front of a group.

Attitude seems to me to be the sum total of all those personal factors we discussed in "You Are the Message." Attitude determines your altitude. Attitude carries you through rain or sleet, high winds and snow.

Technique is the how. How do you go about selling? How do you present yourself? How do you give a presentation? How do you close? Improve your technique and you'll improve the results of the presentations you make.

PRESENTATIONS

Manfred Esser came to the United States from Germany with an idea and a driving ambition. He knew no English so he bought fifteen German-English dictionaries. He placed the books in convenient places so he'd always have one to refer to.

Manfred understood the importance of *activity,* meaning presentations. In a few years Manfred Esser had built a party-plan wine company into a company with sales of more than $25 million. Using the party-plan technique, the company's face-to-face salespeople sold fine wines. Today Manfred is president of and partner in a prestigious winery in California.

Here was a man who came to a new country understanding neither its culture nor its language. Manfred's exceptional tenacity both in learning the language and in making more sales presentations enabled him to succeed against all odds.

Work, the Great Equalizer

Sounds like work? It is. Presentations are work, and work is a great equalizer. It can make you the equal of company presidents, of captains of industry.

As someone said, the average person finds it easier to adjust to failure than to spend the time and effort adjusting to the sacrifices that lead to success.

A Chapter 10 Thought

Prosperity is more than an economic condition; it is a state of mind.

—Frederick Lewis Allen

Remember the lady whose son struck it rich? She found her sales work was fun. She refused to give it up for a life of ease.

Work, in face-to-face sales terms, means presentations. But there's good news about presentations. If you'll just make enough of them, they get you the results—the income—you want. The house in the country, too. The Mercedes. The family helicopter. You name it.

Obvious? Of course. But you'd be amazed if you knew how many face-to-face sellers give up before they learn this simple point. They look around at others and decide they don't have some necessary assets that others have. They assume that means they're programmed to fail.

Nonsense. We've seen the successful face-to-face people come in all shapes and sizes, from all kinds of backgrounds, from families large, medium-sized, and small.

Herbert Casson, a British writer, had another answer. Proving that anyone could learn to sell, Casson wrote:

"In the past ten generations you have had 1,024 ancestors. In the past twenty generations, you have had 1,048,576 ancestors. Therefore you needn't worry about what is 'born' in you. There's plenty of good and bad!"

Putting the Law of Averages to Work

When you go out to make presentations, remember that you're taking the law of averages along with you as a working companion. It will do a tremendous job of helping to make your work productive. Yes, the law of averages can work for you. Let me explain.

Suppose you go off to work and make a string of presentations. You find after a while that you're averaging about one sale for every six presentations. That's a very useful piece of information. Now you know how many presentations you have to make to get the number of sales you need.

You also know that as long as you make those presentations, you will get those sales. Believe me, you will.

You may have to make three times as many presentations as the whiz who picks up one sale for every two presentations. But if you have the energy and the motivation to work hard enough—to make enough presentations—you could end up with more sales than he or she makes.

That's the magic of the law of averages.

Of course, you can turn the telescope around. Look at presentations from the other end. That means you can count your rejections and know that the more there are, the more sales you've made. You don't have to set yourself up as a pessimist in taking this approach. You're simply looking at the law of averages from the other side.

Write It Down!

We've talked about record keeping. Now you can see another reason why it's so important. Unless you have a record of your work, you won't know what your average sales-to-presentations ratio is.

Keeping records may do something else for you. It may remind you that you've done shockingly little work in the past few days or weeks.

I've found that I have to do, every day, things that are directly related to generating business. The questions are always these: On this particular day, have I sold someone, have I recruited someone to sell, or have I taught someone to sell?

I like this daily reminder. I carry it with me each day, and it plays an important part in keeping me on track.

DO IT NOW

Day _____ Date _____

I. MUST DO

1. _____

2. _____

3. _____

4. _____

5. _____

6. _____

7. _____

II. IMPORTANT

1. _____

2. _____

3. _____

4. _____

5. _____

6. _____

7. _____

Would you dare to carry a stopwatch on your selling calls to find out how much time you actually spend in front of prospects in a week or a month? You might be shocked.

How the Law Works...

You could graph it. You could show how the law of averages worked on fifty presentations made by a single face-to-face salesperson. You'd see, in one typical case from one selling field, that the average ratio of success was one in five.

But the presentations that work will never be one in every consecutive batch of five.

Either way you look at it, the law of averages will work for you.

In a typical series of fifty presentations (see the following Sales Progress Chart), the first generated a sale. Then came a dry spell. In twelve presentations, the salesperson garnered no successes at all. A lot of brand-new salespeople would quit at this point. They'd say, "Im just not cut out for this business. Too many No Sales and not enough Sales."

The more experienced salesperson hangs in there. He or she knows the law of averages will work its magic in time. In the preceding case, a streak of five sales was waiting in the next seven presentations. The inexperienced person would have left just in time to miss the feast.

SALES PROGRESS CHART				
1 S	2 NS	3 NS	4 NS	5 NS
6 NS	7 NS	8 NS	9 NS	10 NS
11 NS	12 NS	13 NS	14 S	15 NS
16 S	17 S	18 NS	19 S	20 S
21 NS	22 NS	23 NS	24 NS	25 NS
26 NS	27 NS	28 S	29 NS	30 NS
31 NS	32 NS	33 S	34 NS	35 NS
36 NS	37 NS	38 NS	39 S	40 NS
41 NS	42 NS	43 NS	44 NS	45 NS
46 NS	47 S	48 NS	49 NS	50 NS
S = Sales NS = No Sale				

One way to look at the law of averages: Remind yourself that in a sense you're "paying" for each win with a certain number of losses. If you average one win in five tries, every four losses will entitle you to one win. This illustration is typical of the way the law of averages works in one-on-one selling, but it is also relevant to party-plan selling. It's not as much for all or nothing, but it comes into play in *scheduling* and *show size*.

When working the phone for shows, you may get a lot of no's, but the more calls you make, the more yes's you get. With show size, if your average show is $400, it doesn't mean every show is $400. Some are $100, others $1,000.

... and Works

To go back to one-on-one selling, if you have a string of twelve failures, don't look at it as a disaster. Look forward with pleasure and anticipation to the three wins you've earned.

Because it will continue to work.

Some experienced, expert salespeople with a good product get that proportion of wins and losses down to one in two. That does not mean these salespeople sell every second prospect. It does mean that forty sales will result from 80 presentations.

These are not hypothetical examples. They are reality. Both come from actual records. The first example dates back to an early point in my career when I was getting ten sales for every fifty presentations. At the time I was studying the techniques of some other salespeople who were getting one sale out of every two or three tries.

The second example—one in two—comes from five years later in my career. I had benefited from the learning curve.

As I look back on my own progress in sales I realize that I reached my targets because I made lots of presentations.

Sounds simple? It is. It's as simple as the secret of the man who built a sales staff that sold $30 million worth of water purifiers a year. Asked what he teaches his salespeople about the tcchnical points of the product or proccss he says "I tell them to say that the product works well and the water tastes good."

Who Am I?

I am the foundation of all business. I am the fount of all prosperity. I am the parent of genius. I have laid the ground-work for every fortune ...from [that of] the Rockefellers down.

I must be loved before I can bestow my greatest bless-ings and achieve my greatest ends. Loved, I make life pur-poseful and fruitful. I can do more to advance a youth than his own parents, be they ever so rich.

Fools hate me. Wise men love me. I am represented in every loaf of bread that comes from the oven, in every train that crosses the continent, in every newspaper that comes off the press. I am the mother of democracy. All progress springs from me. Who am I? What am I? I am Work.

—From Ohio Mason

From my own experience I've evolved one basic rule of thumb as follows:

Before Going Home, Make One More Sales Call

Successful salespeople in all fields use this approach. They may be ready to quit for the day and go home. But they have a few minutes left. They make one more call and guess what, another sale.

Ed Benzing, an old friend, may be the perfect example of this spirit. He was managing and training salespeople in the San Antonio, Texas area. He signed all his sales bulletins with this "Spanish" touch:

"Juan Mor Dem." One more demonstration.

In this way he reminded his salespeople that it always pays to make "one more dem."

Think Quantity, Think Time

Nothing can be more important to your success than the sheer numbers of "people you tell your story to." I don't mean to imply that the quality of your presentation isn't important. It is. The ratio of successful presentations to losses will certainly rise as you improve your attitude and your technique.

But real improvement may take some time and practice. Meanwhile, you can do a lot of selling just by doing a heck of a lot of presenting.

Presentations, to me, are like having a money machine in your basement. That machine may be capable of turning out authentic $100 bills. But it's useless until you turn it on.

Think time, too. Beginners in face-to-face selling have excused their lack of presentations by saying that "the prospect will be there tomorrow."

That may or may not be true. What is a fact is this: Put off making presentations, or one more demonstration, and success in selling won't wait for you. It'll take off with someone else.

Remember that poem that spelled out what happens to those who wait?

Now Write It Down

Make presentations *now,* even deadly dull, boring ones. You can count on getting sales.

Can't Afford

The bride, white of hair, stoops over her cane,
Her footsteps uncertain need guiding,
While down the church aisle,
With a wan toothless smile,
The groom in a wheelchair comes riding.
And who is this elderly couple thus wed?
You will find when you've closely explored it,
That here is that rare, most conservative pair,
Who waited till they could afford it.

I'm not recommending boring presentations, you understand. I'm only saying that if that's your present style, you can count on getting some sales.

To make sure you follow through, write down in the following spaces as many action ideas as you can think of—ideas you've generated during this discussion of presentations. All of them should be ideas that you plan to start putting to work immediately.

1. _____

2. _____

3. _____

4. _____

Improving Your Average

You can get good results simply by making a lot of presentations. But, in the long run, it's easier to make more effective presentations. And that boils down to improving your technique.

One sure way to improve your technique is to *close* more often. Look at this example:

Number of sales required 5

Ratio of sales to presentations .... 1 in 5

Number of closes made per presentation 3

Total number of closes required to make five sales 75

Total number of presentations required 25

In the above, you'll have to make twenty-five presentations and a total of seventy-five attempts to close in order to get five sales. However, my own experience has shown me that, if you make more closes, you can reduce the number of presentations and still get the five sales. For example, if you increase the number of closes per presentation to five, you'll get the following picture:

Number of sales required 5

Ratio of sales to presentations .... 1 in 3

Number of closes per presentation 5

Total number of closes required to make five sales 75

Total number of presentations required 15

Result: You've cut your presentations from twenty five to fifteen, and you're still getting five sales!

ATTITUDE

We've got to talk now about A for Attitude, the second letter in the PAT formula. Up to this point, we have stressed how important presentations are in getting lots of sales. Presentations are vital but so is attitude. If you work like a whirlwind but work with a poor *attitude,* with a lack of enthusiasm, you will be a drudge. Working with a strong, positive attitude will make your presentations far more effective and produce much greater results. You'll chalk up a lot more S's on your sales progress chart.

Instead of getting one S for every 5 presentations, you will find yourself getting one S for every three or four presentations.

You can see it happening every day of the week. Two salespeople of equal talent make comparable numbers of presentations. Their product knowledge and skills don't differ greatly, but one of them sells twice as much as the other. Obviously, *attitude* makes the difference.

Let's look more closely at this thing called attitude.

Are You Hard to Sell?

The first and most important point that I want to make about attitude is this: if you're going to be good at selling, you have to be good at buying.

You don't have to squander the grocery money. But it's true that successful people don't have to be sold on everything. They don't sit back with an air of skepticism about every program the company introduces and say, "Prove it." More often they say, "This idea sounds good, and it can work for me. In fact, maybe I can do an exceptional job with it."

Make Things Happen!

You may have noticed it; I've seen it hundreds of times—experience in direct selling dramatically increases a person's "can do" attitude in other areas of life.

What is the change that takes place? You begin to realize that if you concentrate on your *expectations of good things,* rather than worry about the possibility of bad, you can make things happen the way you want them to.

You won't forever be asking, *"What if* something bad happens?" You will be saying, "I'm going to make something good happen."

As though you were a ballplayer chasing a fly ball, you'll say, "If there's a way I can get to it, I'll catch it," not, "What if I drop the ball?"

Don't Kid Yourself About Your Presentations

As I've said, presentations are W-O-R-K. More than anything else, your success will depend on how many hours you spend in front of prospects.

Grab your trusty pencil again and get ready to be ruthlessly honest with yourself. Check your answers to the following when you're quite sure no one is looking over your shoulder.

1) So far this week, about how many hours have you spent in front of a prospect?

   2-5   6-10   11-15   16 or more

2) Last week?

   2-5   6-10   11-15   16 or more

3) What's your daily average?

   1-2   3-4   5-6   7 or more

4) On a typical day, how many breaks do you take for coffee, lunch, personal business, or just plain loafing?

   1-2   3-4   5-6   7 or more

5) How long is your average break?

   5 min   10 min.   15 min.   20 min. or more

Summary: On an average day, you spend _____ hours in front of prospects and _____ hours taking breaks.

You Are What You Think You Are

What's your attitude toward yourself? That's the most important question you have to answer.

Pick up that pencil of yours again and jot down the following (be honest—no one's looking):

1) The three things I like *most* about myself are:_____

_____

_____

_____

_____

2) The three things I like *least* about myself are: _____

_____

_____

_____

_____

3) On a scale of 1 to 10, I rate myself:

    1 2 3 4 5 6 7 8 9 10

4) On a scale of 1 to 10, other people would rate me:

    1 2 3 4 5 6 7 8 9 10

Obviously, there are no right or wrong answers to any of the above. But by doing this you can measure your own attitude toward yourself. *Then* you can give some thought to what you may want to change.

But again, remember: We can change some things about ourselves. Other things we can't change. Know the difference and do what you can.

Oddly enough, most of the time what we think of ourselves determines what other people think of us. Whatever that self-image happens to be is the message we project to others. If your self-image is a good one, they will think highly of you.

And vice versa.

Building on Your Strengths

Consider the stories of two face-to-face sellers, Mary and Carol. Mary was sixty-two, Carol twenty-three. Both were extremely successful salespeople.

Their attitudes impressed everyone who came into contact with them.

Both women worked in units that included salespeople whose ages ranged as far apart as those of Mary and Carol. But as their managers told it, their success boiled down to one very simple principle:

*Build your own strengths and **never** compare your weaknesses to others' strengths.*

Think about this for a minute. At age sixty-two, Mary could have compared herself to the twenty three-year-olds in her group. She could have said, "At sixty-two, I'm too old for this game. I'll never be able to compete with those younger women."

She said nothing of the kind. Instead, she took this attitude: "I'm sixty-two. That means I've got a lot more years of accumulated wisdom than those young greenhorns. I'm bound to have more credibility with prospects than a kid who's wet behind the ears."

And Carol, she could have said, "I just don't have the experience to make a success of this job." But she didn't. She said, instead, "I'm only 23. I've got three times the energy of those older people. I know I can out-work them. I'll show 'em!"

The result? Both were consistent winners. They built on their own particular strengths.

You've Got Something Special

Thomas Jefferson once said, "I've never met a man who couldn't do *something* better than I can." Coming from a man with an extraordinary wide range of talents, that's a remarkable admission.

Jefferson recognized that *everyone* has something special going on for him or her.

What are your strengths? Take a minute and note them down...

_____

_____

_____

_____

_____

_____

_____

_____

_____

_____

_____

_____

_____

_____

Add an appendix if you need one. And next time you start feeling inferior to someone, just recall what you wrote above.

Now let's review what we've said in previous chapters about attitude...

- Attitude is a very important part of success and can often overcome a lack of knowledge and extensive training.

- Avoid negative people like the plague. Their attitudes are horribly contagious.

- Cultivate positive, "rainy day" people.

- Set specific goals—but avoid the goal-setting pitfalls. (If you can't remember them, go back to chapter 4 and refresh your memory.)

- Plan a life agenda.

- Keep the luster in your daily living by reading or listening to inspirational materials.

- Self-image is your most important asset. Know your strengths and weaknesses, but never compare your weaknesses to someone else's strengths.

Action Ideas

Action encourages action. On the lines below, or on a separate sheet of paper, write as many action ideas as you can think of—ideas that occurred to you during this discussion of attitude. These should be ideas that you plan to start using immediately.

_____

_____

_____

_____

_____

_____

_____

_____

_____

_____

_____

_____

_____

_____

_____

_____

_____

TECHNIQUE

Up to now, we've talked in this chapter about the importance of making lots of presentations even lousy ones, to keep
the law of averages working for you. We've talked, too, about
how your attitude can help make the most of every opportunity as well as communicate a positive attitude to others.

Now I'd like to talk about the third letter in PAT—the
letter T. It stands, as you know, for Technique, an element in
selling that offers you tremendous leverage for maximizing
your performance.

Much of this book is about technique.

But think of this:

In the area of technique, you can set yourself the task of
deliberately improving your law of averages ratio so that you
get more sales with fewer presentations.

Here's my favorite story on the importance of technique.

A large machine in an industrial plant stopped working. The plant manager had his own mechanic try to fix it, with no luck. Finally, he called in an expert from the other side of town. The expert looked at the machine for about two minutes and then tapped on it in a certain place. It began working.

When the bill arrived, it was for $100. The plant manager thought the bill was unreasonable for two minutes' work, so he asked for an itemized bill.

His request was answered promptly. The new bill read:

Tapping on machine $1.00

Knowing where to tap 99.00

I'd agree. If you know where to tap, your results will improve tremendously.

How you say it is important! Technique is a matter of semantics—the words you use can make a difference.

Once Again, Keep Track

You can't keep track this week and forget about it next week. Your records will be a shambles. You won't know whether you are improving from one sale in five or six presentations to one in three or four—or whether you're improving at all.

Suppose you've passed through that hardest door of all to get through—your own. Assume you've done your homework. You have a prospect, you make a presentation. You chalk up a success.

Really chalk it up. Make a note, quickly, using whatever system you've adopted. Record keeping is another part of technique, one that enables you to say, "On such and such a day I was this much closer to my goal."

How you say it is important! Technique is a matter of semantics—the words you use can make a difference.

Say this:	Not this:
1) Your neighbors, the Joneses, are the proud owners of our program.	I sold the Joneses this program.
2) You will enjoy evaluating this program.	I'd like to demonstrate this product to you.
3) I have a couple of exciting ideas I'm anxious to share with you.	I'd like to explain some of the features of our product to you.
4) Here are some facts that you may find meaningful.	I'll be honest with you.
5) Does this explanation make sense?	Do you follow me?
6) For a total investment of	For a cost of
7) I'll need your OK right here.	Your signature is required here.
8) You have the privilege of carrying this as long as thirty months if you choose.	Your payments will run for two and one-half years at this rate.
9) What sort of deposit would you like to put on this today?	How large a down payment would you like to make?
10) The best part of this is how easy it is to own. It is only this amount (point to amount on order pad).	The cost is only four hundred and ninety-nine dollars.
11) The service charge is only a penny and a half per dollar on the unpaid balance.	The interest is 1-1/2% a month.
12) The session that you have an opportunity to attend is an Evaluation Seminar; it's an opportunity for you to evaluate [the product or opportunity].	I'd like you to come to our sales training workshop.

SUMMARY

When I first started in sales, I heard a lot of jargon. Some seemed to be pure mumbo-jumbo. I was expected to learn specific "steps to the sale," terms like "Resolve to Buy" and "Affirmation Steps," etc.

I had trouble understanding some of those terms.

I know today that a few fundamental things should happen on the way to a sale. If you do these things, you make things happen. There are seven of them.

Here they are:

1) Get a prospect

2) Get in front of the prospect

3) Build rapport and qualify the prospect

4) Know the product or service

5) Close the process

6) Seal the sale

7) Get more prospects

Write them down. Carry them next to your list of achievements.

The PAT success formula will never fail you in selling. If you are not succeeding, you can bet that one of the three ingredients—Presentation, Attitude, or Technique—is missing from what you are doing. ❏

CHAPTER ELEVEN

Group Selling

hat is "group selling?" A definition: "Group selling is a sales situation in which you sell your product, service, or idea to more than one person at a time. The product you sell may be original art such as my own company sells in a "home show" setting. It might be a typical "party plan" product line such as Tupperware or Mary Kay. Or it might be a time-sharing real estate product.

On the other hand the item(s) you're selling might be an *idea*, such as joining a direct-selling company. The group selling would take place as an "opportunity night" or "evaluation seminar" or some other recruiting event.

The Advantages of Selling to Groups

Group selling has a number of significant advantages over one-on-one selling. These advantages are probably apparent to me in particular because I spent a big part of my career selling one-on-one.

Some of these advantages are:

- Time efficiency—multiple sales
- Group enthusiasm—consensus
- Appeal to a mix of people
- Easy prospecting
- Reduced pressure to buy

Let's look at these advantages in more detail.

Time Efficiency—Multiple Sales

When you make individual sales calls, you are only going to be able to "get in front of" a certain number of prospects each day and each week. I recently questioned a number of successful real estate people (who sell both residential and commercial property) about the number of prospects per week that they actually take out to look at properties. I was surprised to learn that they averaged only three or four per week.

Whether you, as a "one-on-one salesperson," get in front of three or four prospects per week or three or four per day, your sales volume and income are limited by that number. In contrast, group selling allows you to get in front of a number of people at once. The possibility of bigger sales volume and more commissions is obvious.

Group Enthusiasm—Consensus

Did you ever attend a sales meeting on an evening when a sudden snowstorm developed, and only you and your manager showed up? If you did, you might have noticed that the applause was not as loud as usual. If your sales had been exceptional the previous week, you may have been a little "let down" by the lack of "stroking" that you usually get from all your colleagues who usually attend the meetings.

True, it's tough to whip up a frenzy of enthusiasm at such an event without a number of people in attendance. On the

r hand, the enthusiasm generated by a few people in a
n who "get into" a situation or a line of products is totally
tagious.

At a typical home show or party, one or more of the guests,
addition to the host or hostess, may have been to one of
iese events before. They are probably enjoying the products
nd will therefore offer powerful testimonials. Even better,
hey will usually make additional purchases. The atmosphere
it such a function is one where a positive buying climate
exists because there is a consensus that "this is the right thing
to do." Also, previously satisfied customers provide a security
blanket to the other guests in the audience. They help to
remove any suspicion that might exist. When a salesperson
says something, his or her motivation for saying it is self-
serving. When a customer says the product is absolutely
fabulous, the rest of the guests are convinced.

I keep running across evidence of how potent this "proper
buying climate" can be. As one of our salespeople told me, "The
hostess at one of my parties warned me that two of the guests
were not going to buy. But they wanted to attend anyway.
Before the party was over, the hostess had bought eight
paintings, and the two 'nonbuyers' had purchased two paintings each—and apologized for not buying more."

This is an environment in which you have the tremendous
advantage of facing people in the room who are "presold."
They will often do a better selling job on the other guests than
you could do.

Appeal to a Mix of People

If your product line offers a wide range of products and you
demonstrate these products to me, I may want to own one or
more, but it is unlikely that I am going to want to purchase a
large selection. If a group of people attend a session together
to see that same product line, most of them will probably
purchase more than one of those products.

The group-selling situation not only benefits from the
differing tastes of the people who make up the group but from

their differing personalities. The less outgoing or slow-to-act people often move more quickly than usual. They become buyers at such an event because they get excited and are motivated by other outgoing, enthusiastic guests.

Easy Prospecting

My particular business offers an excellent opportunity both for people who want to use the group-sales process and for people who wish to make one-on-one sales by calling on businesses. One of our most productive salespeople (who enjoys a six-figure income) is often asked why she doesn't make one-on-one business calls. All her sales efforts go into conducting art shows in homes.

She replies with a lot of conviction that the system she uses ensures that she never needs to worry about where her next sales call will be. Like any effective group seller, she usually schedules one or more new shows from every show she conducts. Her average show has eight or ten guests, so she has eight or ten people who are prospective hosts or hostesses at her next show.

Reduced Pressure to Buy

Many people who attend a group-sales function go there with the intention of not buying anything. Their notion that they will just attend but not buy may be based on a variety of reasons: lack of money, prejudice against the product line, and so on. These negative assumptions are often strong enough that they would not consider subjecting themselves to a one-on-one sales presentation. They assume that the group will give them enough obscurity to avoid any sales pressure.

What really happens is that when they attend the party or show, the law of averages works in favor of the salesperson. The hesitant prospect is frequently the biggest buyer in the group.

Special Techniques for Group Selling

The first thing that needs to be made clear when discussing sales techniques for group selling is that most of the principles used in one-on-one selling are relevant to group selling. The "sales process" we have already discussed is applicable. There are, however, nuances of group selling that you should be tuned in to. Here are a few tips:

1. Make the most of the physical setting
2. Pre-sell your host or hostess
3. Know the makeup of your group
4. Speak to the individuals in the group
5. Know how to handle negative guests

Now let's look at each of these points in more detail.

Physical Setting

The setting for your group selling may be less than ideal. You may think you can't do anything to improve it.

It's true, of course, that if you are invited to do a party or show in a very small apartment, you can't make it bigger. But you can recognize one advantage that a small setting provides—increased intimacy. There is no question that in a room full of people more enthusiasm can usually be generated than in a large room that is sparsely populated.

If your selling space is large, you need to impress upon your hostess the importance of a large guest list.

Each type of group selling will require a different physical setting. Lighting, tables for the demonstrator, and seating arrangements for the guests will probably be different for each product line. The important thing is that you make the best of the space and furnishings you have in order to enhance your group-selling situation. Most party-plan sellers make their presentation from the "focal point" in the room—usually in front of the TV set. Working in front of the TV also prevents it from being turned on and becoming a distraction.

Pre-Sell Your Host, Hostess, or a Key Person in the Group

It has already been emphasized that you need to recruit an enthusiastic guest. If you do your job effectively, your host client should be your sales partner for the day or evening. But remember: Everything is a selling job; this is no exception.

Hopefully, your host/hostess will be enthusiastic about your product line and the sales event he or she has agreed to host for you. But it's up to you to maximize that enthusiasm, to do everything necessary to "excite" this person. Sell him or her on the fact that this is your business and that you want the party or show to be one of the best you have ever had.

Always remind your hosts of what's in it for them—which is usually a lot. Free products, product discounts, and their own enhanced reputation as people capable of doing a good job—these are some of the obvious rewards.

Your preparation and coaching of your key people will determine how well they do. Show attendance, the enthusiasm of the group, and the relaxed buying climate necessary for success will all be the results of the quality of the "selling job" you have done with these important people. If your group-selling event is not in a typical party-plan setting, or if it is not hosted by a single person, you probably can still get a similar advantage from one or more of the guests. For example, in a group-recruiting event, you will usually have a number of guests who you will know are "presold" on joining your organization. You can coach them to give some form of a testimonial or to be an early "decision maker" at the event.

This brings us to the next major point.

Know the Makeup of Your Group

The specific products that you highlight, the particular features of your products that you stress, or the third-person stories you use in your sales presentation will be determined by *what you know about the individuals* who attend your group presentation. The salesperson who does a good job of getting as much information as possible about the guests before the presentation has a major advantage and will get better results.

We just discussed the importance of the hostess, host, or key person. This person can give you valuable information about the people who have been invited, but you need to *ask*. The next opportunity to find out more about the guests is to be genuinely interested in them when you meet them. In the typical party or home show, a number of the guests arrive early. This gives you a special opportunity to get a feel for what they think of your product or service as well as allowing you to establish a rapport with them.

Make certain you are introduced to them when they arrive. In a relaxed, friendly manner, if you don't already know the answer, ask them what they know about your product or service and determine their degree of receptivity.

Speak to the Individuals in the Group

Some prospective salespeople are skeptical about succeeding in group selling because they aren't accomplished public speakers. A member of my company's sales team with a $100,000-plus annual income is honestly terrified of speaking before a group of her peers at a routine sales meeting. In spite of this, she consistently gets spectacular results in front of groups of five, ten, or twenty people in homes—selling our paintings.

This super salesperson is totally comfortable and confident in this setting because *she knows her topic* exceptionally well. She has a conviction about her products and her mission, and she has shared this particular message many times. This superseller's conviction comes from experience. She has been getting wonderful feedback from her customers for years. She believes in what she sells. She also knows what she's going to say, what props to use, what products she will show.

She even has ideas for getting the audience involved. For example, she learns from the hostess that Michelle Brown loves to help out, loves to be the center of attention. The superseller will definitely bring Michelle into the presentation at the right point.

I have a reason for mentioning the concern that many people have when they are new to the selling business: If you're going to be tuned in to the *individulals in the group,* you can't be worrying about how you are doing. Just remember that although you're talking to more than one person, you are talking to a bunch of *nice people.* You are talking to them one person at a time, and they are listening to you as if you are talking to them as individuals.

Just remember too that if you are really into your business, you probably won't be uptight. After all, fear and enthusiasm don't mix.

There's another reason to tune in to the individual in the group: for validation of your product.

As I mentioned, you will be concentrating on "talking, communicating, and selling" to these people. You will have some guests who are enthusiastic owners of your products. It's essential that you have them *validated* the *quality, value,* and *benefits* of those products. You'll say things like, "Mary, this painting is the same type of wildlife scene that you bought for your husband's den, isn't it? That painting really did add a wonderful touch to the room, didn't it?"

You know Mary well enough to be sure she will gush about how wonderful the painting is—even after your obviously rhetorical question. You know the individuals well enough to pick out the right ones to ask specific questions.

Another way of tuning in to the individuals is to have frequent eye contact with guests in various parts of the room. Be careful not to neglect any of the guests. When you establish good eye contact you will be having a *conversation* with an individual—even when you don't ask questions or call him or her by name.

The impact of eye contact was brought home to me recently when one of my four-year-old twin daughters was showing me pictures taken at her summer camp six months earlier. A member of the Chicago Bears football team an offensive lineman who is not well known, was a luncheon guest at the camp. Four-year-old Molly pointed him out in a snapshot and said proudly "This is John Smith and when he was talking he kept looking at me."

When a four-year-old is flattered by eye contact and the memory sticks for six months I think it proves my point.

Good Eye Contact—An Effective Way To Reach Your Guests *Speaking to people by name is another way to tune in to your group.* Nothing is more flattering to an individual in a group than to be a spoken to by name. The more guests in attendance, the more flattering it is. It says to the guest "You count." The guest responds by thinking,

"Wow the 'presenter' has just met me and remembers my name. I must have made a favorable impression." And: "I'm important to him (her)."

How often do you hear people say "I'm terrible at remembering names"? *Well, you don't need to be terrible at remembering names.* Decide to work at being *good* at remembering names! It will make you more effective and will increase your sales. Here are a few tips on how to remember names at a home show.

Greet each guest as he or she arrives. We have already pointed out the importance of getting to know them when they arrive. But a most important part of this greeting is making sure you have their names right and letting them sink into your brain. When you are introduced, use each name in your greeting. An example: "It's nice to meet you, Mary."

Use the name in conversation. Greeting guests as they arrive for your show, you can often find ways to comment about their names. For example, you might say, "Hello, Evelyn. I have a sister Evelyn."

By mentioning a name several times in conversation or, even better, by commenting on it, your chances of remembering it will increase dramatically.

Make a chart. Another practical thing you can do is to make a chart of the room in advance. When the guests introduce themselves to the group, jot the names down and keep the chart where you can refer to it as a reminder. You'll find this prop a big help.

Pass out name tags. The tags of course, identify the members of the group—especially if you write the first names in big letters. If you are preparing the name tags and giving them to the guests, it gives you another opportunity to practice their names and use them in conversation.

Know How to Handle Negative Guests

Part of being "tuned in" is all awareness of the possibility that you may have guests who are not assets to your "selling situation." How do you handle the negative person in the group? First, it's important to remember that there are a number of reasons why the person might be negative. It could be because the individual has a "can't afford" problem and therefore "puts down" your products to save face. Or the person might feel that a parent, spouse, or relative in the group has been carried away with your presentation and is overspending.

Whatever the reason, it will help you if you recognize that negativeness is usually not a rejection of you but probably a reaction to a situation over which you have no control.

Secondly, in dealing with the negative person it's essential that you avoid a confrontation. Otherwise the rest of the group will feel compelled to defend the negative person. You could win the battle and lose the war.

If the negative person attacks one of your products, and your product line consists of a lot of products, you might say, "It would be a dull world if we all liked the same thing. We have 125 products, and even I'll admit I'm not wild about *all* of them."

If your company has a guarantee of satisfaction, you can remind all the guests of this. If you can say that you or the company will take back any product if they aren't satisfied, that will defuse the situation. To a guest who complains about poor customer service or a defective product they have received, it is also highly effective to say simply, "Would you talk to me as soon as the show is over? We can solve that." or "We'll clear that up."

Another thing you can do is bring the critics into your presentation. Involve them. Get their opinions regarding the best way to explain some of your products. Your special attention will often bring them around.

Answers to Questions About Group Selling

1) Is there an ideal time for a group presentation? How long should such a presentation run?

   A: The time involved in making a presentation will vary. Most people feel that forty-five to sixty minutes is about as long as you can go without losing your audience. If you're closing individuals on the spot, that can take at least another hour. But in the final hour, the attendees can enjoy refreshments. There can be a real party atmosphere. The answer to the time question is again one where common sense and good judgment have to prevail.

2) Can you start a presentation or demonstration with a warmup?

   A: Yes, definitely. A lot of top salespeople start by asking the guests one at a time to introduce themselves. They may also ask them to say what they like about the products and to describe how they use them.

3) How can you make sure you don't bore your group?

   A: Remember to use movement or change of pace. This can involve going from one item in your product line to another. It can involve physical movement. Also remember that you can involve the members of the group. You may bring in your host or hostess to give a testimonial on a specific product. You'll invent other ways. The key word is variety.

4) Can you bring a dead group back to life?

   A: Yes. The role of humor is very important. Even if you don't tell good jokes, if you are affable, it will show. And you can ask for questions. One of our best salespersons asks the guests questions throughout her entire presentation. When they don't seem to be "with it," she will tease them by saying, "I may have to give you folks this entire presentation again to be sure you get it!" The down-to-earth approach works wonders.

5) Is it appropriate to send follow-up notes after a group sales event?

A: It can be. I've mentioned in other places in this book some of the situations where follow-up notes are important. Above all, I'd strongly urge that you send a thank-you note to your host or hostess. You may want to write to any members of a group you expect to see again. Or you might want to send a note to a big buyer.

6) How far in advance should you set up a party or home show?

A: In a typical situation, three weeks is ideal. But some salespeople get great results from parties scheduled as little as three days ahead. Your own calendar will determine how far in advance you should schedule. If you have few shows scheduled, book your shows as soon as possible.

7) When should you arrive at the home of your host or hostess?

A: Be practical. Will you have a lot of setting up to do? You may want to be on the spot an hour before your starting time. If you have little or no setting up to do, twenty or thirty minutes might be sufficient. In all circumstances, your host or hostess should know what time you'll be arriving.

8) Are there other types of rewards or premiums for the host or hostess aside from those previously mentioned?

A: There usually are. The rewards the hostess gets usually depend on the success of the show or party. Success is determined by sales volume and future shows scheduled.

9) What are the limits on the earnings of group salespeople?

A: There's no real limit. It depends on how much time and work you are willing to put into the business and how effective you become. There are people in group selling who are earning as much as $300,000 or $400,000 a year.

10) Are you always recruiting at a group sales function?

A: Yes. But see my chapter on recruiting (chapter 12).

SUMMARY

The whole idea in group selling is that effective use of the tools and techniques I've shared with you will make every individual in the group feel "engaged" in the process. The result will be that you will realize the rewards of your efforts at the end of the evening—when you total up your sales.

Remember the basic steps:

1) Do the best job you can with the physical setting you have.

2) Make your hostess your "sales partner" for the evening.

3) Know the makeup of your group.

4) Speak to the individuals in the group.

5) Know how to handle negative guests. Above all—*give a great presentation.*

Giving a great presentation involves all the points we've just made, but it's much more. It's really *being "up" for what you are doing.* It's deciding that you have an exciting message and quality products to introduce to your guests. You need to believe in your heart that the people who attend your show or party are very fortunate to be able to learn about your products or service. It is also knowing they will really benefit by becoming customers. So you are there to do business, and you make outstanding things happen.

Finally, you need to rememher that a top priority of your sales process is to schedule additional shows. In addition to getting sales, you also need to share the opportunity with others and persuade them to join your company. You are on your way. ❏

CHAPTER TWELVE

Recruiting

e have said it before: *Everything* is a selling job. It's certainly true of recruiting. Even if you're not involved in selling to earn a living or supplement your income, recruiting skills can be a tremendous asset. Just like sales skills, recruiting skills—your ability to attract people to what you are doing and to bring them to want to join you or your group—will be a wonderful benefit to you.

The Importance of Recruiting Skills

I want to make this specific. If you're in sales, part- or fulltime, recruiting skills can make you the most valuable person on a sales team.

Let's say you sell $100,000 for the year, and the entire sales team sells $1,000,000; you're responsible for 10 percent of the team's volume. If, however, you sell the same amount but also recruit five other people whose part-time sales efforts produce an additional $100,000, your contribution to the team's sales and profits has doubled. You have become twice as valuable to the team. In most companies, your income would increase proportionally.

Although compensation programs vary from company to company, and requirements for qualification for earning manager status and overrides differ, in most cases you would get an impressive increase in income because of your recruiting results.

Become a Recruiter and Perform Miracles

Although your personal accomplishments in sales can be outstanding, the results that you can achieve through enlisting the efforts of others can appear to be miraculous. The same is true of your income potential.

Most successful sales organizations have compensation plans that make it possible for an individual to remove all limits from his or her income potential through recruiting and building sales teams.

Think about this for a moment. If you are selling a big-ticket item, and top performance in your company is selling one unit per day, it is unlikely that you are going to be able to double or triple that performance next year or the year after. But if you are increasing your income through recruiting, it can be done. You have removed the limitations that the number of hours in a day puts on you when you are depending solely on your own efforts.

There are other advantages to getting involved in recruiting and team building. You broaden the scope of your work and make it more interesting, for example. When you are working with new people, your job will have more facets to it, and you're less apt to get jaded or suffer burnout.

There's more. The excitement and enthusiasm of new people are contagious and may be the shot in the arm that you need. Sometimes your recruits will fan your competitive flame to ensure that you won't be outdone by these fresh upstarts.

So, as you can see, there are a lot of reasons why you need to become a recruiter.

Activity vs. Ability

Can I be good at recruiting? It is possible that you are not even asking this question. Maybe you've tried recruiting and have already decided that you aren't good at it.

Well, if this is the case, change your mind. At least, reopen your mind. You have probably incorrectly prejudged your own talents in this area.

First of all, recruiting is *no different* from selling. The same basic skills and the same parts of the *sales process* you use in selling also work in recruiting. As with everything else in sales, *attitude* is the key ingredient. So often, people who tell me that they aren't "good at recruiting" admit that this opinion is based on the fact that they had two or three or four recruiting prospects and they all "fell through"—or they "tried it and it didn't work out."

On the other hand, they may have recruited several prospects and *only one* of those prospects joined the company. I usually inform them that their efforts are as good as or better than most "successful recruiters" in the company. Their only problem was that they hadn't done enough recruiting activity to give the law of averages a chance to work.

The first step toward recruiting success is to remove any mental barriers or limitations that you may have already placed on yourself. There is no logical reason why you can't be as effective as the better recruiters in your company.

Now, you ask, how do I go about finding recruits?

Who Do I Want to Recruit?

My conviction that there is always an ample supply of *good people* available to recruit is based on years of experience in several companies with different product lines.

Maybe the term *good people* should be commented on. My daughter Tammy was one of the top distance runners in Illinois in her senior year of high school. A number of fine colleges across the country attempted to *recruit* her. A college coach who attended one of her track meets told me that his institution didn't just look for "good athletes," they looked for "good people." I liked that.

It occurred to me that the same is true when I recruit salespeople. I don't just look for good *salespeople*, I look for *good people*.

As I mentioned before, salespeople are made, not born. This is true, but let me list a few pointers to give you a leg up on recruiting quality prospects for your sales team.

What Traits Do I Look For?

History of success If a recruiting prospect has a history that does not include many successes in life, it is probably overly optimistic to expect that this person is suddenly going to become a successful member of your sales team.

Conversely, a person who has made success a habit, whether it has been in sports, academics, a prior career, or parenting, can probably achieve success in your business.

Strong work ethic I've looked at the backgrounds of many of the successful people I've recruited throughout my career to determine what they had in common. The one constant was their strong work ethic. Frequently, they came from large families with modest financial resources. From childhood, hard work was a necessary and expected part of their lives.

This should not be surprising. If a recruit is a worker, an important part of the basic success formula, PAT—the P for Presentations—will probably get the attention it deserves.

Strong personality By strong personality, I don't mean an extrovert personality; rather, I mean a person who has the ability to project to others his or her conviction about a product or an idea.

Some of the most productive salespeople I've known were basically shy, but they got your attention when they talked to you. They had that important trait—believability. However low-key their manner, you knew they were not wishy-washy individuals. Believability is a quality I look for in every prospective recruit.

Where Will I Find Recruits?

If you buy the idea that lots of good people are available, you then need to determine where to get these recruits. I should point out that there are "experts" who will tell you that recruiting salespeople isn't what it was in the "good old days." Well, I choose to believe that it's the old story of whether the glass is half empty or half full.

An example: One of the excuses used by recruiters who aren't making things happen is that, today, women in America are all working. A few years ago, these people say, "There were an incredible number of women at home taking care of the house and the kids—all *waiting to be recruited* for a part- or full-time sales job."

The first part of this scenario is true. They were home and now they are working. A recent survey showed that 97 percent of American women now expect to work outside the home during their marriage. My reaction is: This is *great,* for two reasons:

1. Many women in this 97 percent could be assets to my business, and they would find a better opportunity as members of my sales team than they could find in other jobs.

2. Even if they already have full-time employment, many of them could enjoy a profitable part-time job with my company.

Now, let's get specific and decide what the primary sources of recruits are.

Personal sphere of influence   Just as in selling, in recruiting the best place to begin is in your own sphere of influence. The old Girard's Rule 250 works. In recruiting you have a wide circle of friends, relatives, neighbors, and business associates who have a high regard for you and will respond positively to your suggestion that they consider joining you in your work. You will probably be surprised at how many of them have already thought about getting involved in your business. In most cases they will be flattered that you asked—even if the time is not right for them to say yes.

The important thing is that you practice the LIBK (Let It Be Known) rule.

Second sale   When you're in front of the prospects, your first priority is to sell your product. However, if you are *working smart,* there is a *second sale* to be made. Regardless of whether or not you've sold the prospect on buying your product, the second sale is recruiting the prospect to join your company.

If the prospect has just bought your product, an important part of the recruiting interview has already been accomplished. If she didn't buy, it may be because she feels she can't afford the product right now. If this is the case, getting involved in sales can be a way she will be able to afford it!

If you're enthusiastic about recruiting and understand the importance of *sharing your opportunities* with a lot of people, the second sale will give you a constant stream of recruiting prospects. It works.

Referrals from recruits   If you're an experienced salesperson, you'll agree that people who have just bought your
product are especially enthusiastic about it. The same is true of
new recruits, people who are tasting the fruits of success in your
business for the first time.

If you ask them to *share the opportunity*—to introduce the
people in their circles of influence to you and the company—they
will sometimes attract recruits in bunches. Just like the second
sale, referrals from recruits or other members of your sales team
will give you a steady supply of recruits if you emphasize
recruiting to them.

Niches especially suited to your business   Every business I've been associated with has been aware of a *niche* of people
who, by vocation or interest, would be "naturals" as prospective
recruits for that particular business.

If a particular group doesn't readily come to mind, brain-
storm this idea with colleagues.

Focus on a special group or groups of people who will make
especially effective recruits for you. For example, consider the
following *niches* in business.

- *Clothing sales*—fashion designers or anyone who loves
  apparel

- *Educational books*—teachers

- *Health care products*—nurses

- *Home enhancement*—interior designers

- *Kitchenware products*—home economists, chefs

- *Cosmetics, personal care products*—hair stylists

This discussion of places to find recruits has barely scratched the surface, only highlighted a few key areas. For example, you might ask, "What about newspaper ads, direct mailings, and so on?" Some books on this subject would lead you to believe that ads are the *primary* source for building a sales team.

My opinion is that the author of such a book either hasn't been active in sales for twenty years or maybe never was. Ads can *supplement* your recruiting efforts, but they probably will not become a primary source. The exception to relying on ads might be when you are looking for one key person in a specific geographic area.

If you concentrate on the key sources as listed above and *think recruiting* all the time, you will find excellent recruiting prospects on a regular basis.

A Recruiting Talk That Recruits

Now that we know where to find recruits, we need to know what to say when we get in front of a prospect. What can you say to motivate a person to join you?

I'm not going to put words in your mouth. Rather, I'm going to stress important points about an effective recruiting talk. These concepts have worked for me in successful recruiting of salespeople in all parts of North America as well as in other parts of the world.

Understand, again, that you are the message The image you project; your enthusiasm, conviction, sincerity, appearance, and manner—all these will have a greater impact on any potential recruit than anything you verbalize. One of the nicest compliments many of my salespeople receive, and it happens often, is from a customer who says, "I saw Mary doing her show, and I could see that she enjoyed what she was doing."

At the same time, if you are succeeding in your business, your success will attract people. I always say to my salespeople, "Don't tell your recruiting prospect what he or she will get from the business, tell them what you get from it!" I know their personal success stories will carry more weight than anything else. Their talk *from the heart* will have a stronger impact than any glossy recruiting brochure.

Personalize your interview Point out to your prospective recruit that you are *exploring* this opportunity with him or her because:

- They showed enthusiasm at your show or during the sales interview.

- Your friend "referred me to you" because he or she felt you were a "natural" for our business.

- "I heard you were thinking of making a career change." (Also, "You can explore the possibility of a career with our company before leaving your present position.")

- "I know you work hard for your present income, and I'm confident you can give yourself a pay raise with us."

Use qualifying questions:

- Could you use an extra $12,000 per year on top of your regular income?

- Do you feel you are worth more than you are presently being paid?

- Are you satisfied with your present career growth?

- When you observed my sales presentation, did you see me do anything that you didn't feel you could do?

Sell specifics of the opportunity Our business meets the needs of people with a wide range of goals. For example:

- X number of shows or presentations per week = Y sales and income.

- Explain compensation program.

- Explain career path for advancement.

- Indicate where you can be five years from now.

Show proof that "the system" works:
- Show a company newsletter with sales figures and success stories.

- Share your own personal success story.

- Show your weekly paychecks, evidence of special awards, other proofs of success.

Add additional value (optional):
- Explain opportunities for *personal growth.*

- Note special meetings, training, conventions, and so on.

- Show brochures of company trips, awards, prizes.

   Close   Ask the potential recruit to make a minor decision at this point to:

- Go on a sales call, attend a party, a sales meeting, or sit in on an opportunity session.

- Use a reservation form to back up this decision.

   My salespeople use a reservation form to *commit* the recruiting prospect to attend a company event. Although signing this form doesn't cost anything, it indicates a very minor decision. It is a stronger psychological commitment than if the prospect had not signed anything.

   Bring the recruit to the event   Personally bringing the recruit to the opportunity session or other event is a very important step in the process. Most recruiting prospects have far greater fears about their ability to do the work than they will tell you. If you arrange to pick them up, the chances that they will get cold feet are greatly reduced.

The second thing that is vital is that you get him or her into a training program *immediately*. Prospective recruits *cool off*. They change their minds, so your attrition rate with prospective recruits will be much lower if you get them started as soon as possible after the recruiting interview.

Group Recruiting Functions

Many direct-selling companies, such as Amway, recruit substantial numbers at group functions that are *specifically recruiting functions*. The functions have different labels, such as Opportunity Nights, Evaluation Seminars, Recruiting Breakfasts, or Sponsor Parties, but they are all recruiting functions.

There are two significant advantages to this type of recruiting. One, every member of the sales team has a good chance to get a recruit or recruits because all they need to do is bring them to the event. If the event is well planned and executed, the recruiting job will be accomplished there. The second advantage is that a tremendous amount of enthusiasm can be generated at the recruiting event by the testimonials of successful salespersons in the organization. Prospective recruits will find it easy to identify with the different personalities they see among these successful people. They see that "ordinary people" like themselves can earn outstanding incomes in the business.

You will find the previous chapter on "Group Selling" helpful if you intend to be involved in group recruiting functions.

SUMMARY

Let me say again that the recruiting process is very similar to the sales process because it's a selling job. For example:

- You find a recruiting prospect.

- You get in front of him or her.

- You build rapport (personalize).

- You sell them (specifics of opportunity).

- You close (get them to attend an event).

- You seal the sale (reassure them). ❑

CHAPTER THIRTEEN

Straight Talk

 top-notch salesperson was helping me get started. The sales interview seemed to flounder when the lady prospect told us she could not buy our product because she believed the world was going to come to an end shortly.

Her belief was based on religious teachings.

My mentor spoke to her softly and respectfully. "I respect your position," he said. "I make it a rule never to question anyone's religious, political, or other very personal beliefs".

"But what if you looked at it this way? What if you bought this product so that Johnny and Mary would have the use of it in the little time remaining to them? You seem convinced that they would enjoy having these books. And when the world comes to an end, you won't have to keep paying for them."

That story illustrates the fact that face-to-face selling requires logic and common sense; it's a never-ending challenge. When you're getting into it, you may have growth pangs. But it's enjoyable even when it's tough. It builds concentration and determination, too, because—if you're like me—you have to force yourself at times to make that "one more dem."

But that has been described as the common denominator of success: forcing yourself to do the things failures are not willing to do.

In this last chapter of the book, I want to share some random items that summarize my philosophy of selling. I hope you'll find some nuggets that will help you prepare for bigger and better things in sales or life in general.

Choosing a Company

At this point, you might ask, "Are you saying that I really can't go wrong if I follow the advice in *Face-to-Face Selling?* If I'm enthusiastic, have enough sales activity, follow the basic techniques required for your particular type of selling, can I just watch the money roll in regardless of the company I join?" No, that's not necessarily true. As pointed out a number of times in the book, most people who fail in sales could make a reasonable case that "it wasn't their fault." The fact remains, however, that they failed. But it is possible to join a company where the chances of succeeding in sales are dramatically reduced. There are pitfalls to avoid. There are always going to be companies out there that should be avoided.

In selecting the right company, here are three vital considerations:

- The company
- The product(s)
- The marketing plan

Let me elaborate briefly:

The company   Sales companies are composed of *people!* The people at the top of the company and at all levels of the company including those in your local area are the best indication of what kind of company it is. Are you impressed with the "kind of people" they are as well as how successful they appear to be?

The next thing to consider is the financial stability of the organization. There are a number of ways you can find information on this aspect of the company. If the company is a direct-selling company, you can check with the Direct Selling Association (DSA) at 1776 K Street N.W., Suite 600, Washington, DC 20006; (202) 293-5760. There is a good chance they will be able to provide you with valuable information.

The product(s)   Is the product or service a proven one? Does it appear that it is the best or one of the best available in the marketplace? Has it been proven to you that it delivers the claims the company makes about it? Does it appear to be reasonably priced? (Remember that a product or service offered by a direct seller can sometimes justifiably cost more because of the personal service provided.) Most importantly, would you be *proud* to sell this product or service?

The marketing plan   Of the three points the "Marketing Plan" is the one that needs most careful scrutiny. Get-rich-quick schemes always seem to be available. I know some fine intelligent people who have been around the direct-selling industry for years who seem to be attracted to such companies. "Red flag" statements that you should watch out for are these:

- *"You don't need to sell anything."*—"All you need to do is steer people to the company and, since you are on the ground floor you will be making tons of money within six months."

My reaction to this—"Baloney!" and I should probably say something even stronger. If there is a legitimate product or service to be sold, someone has to *sell it* and someone needs to train people to sell it. This leads to another caveat.

- *"There is no work involved."*—"After you get the recruiting momentum going, the business will take care of itself." The line goes like this: "Your income from this business will be so big that you will be able to leave the corporate rat race and live a tension-free existence."

Again I say "Baloney!" It's true that a direct-selling career can offer you a rewarding alternative to the stress-filled corporate environment with its politics and pecking order, but I haven't yet seen a lucrative profession that didn't require ongoing hard work.

- *"For a few thousand, you can get a much higher commission rate."* Beware of companies requiring heavy start-up costs.

There are legitimate distributorships that require subtantial amounts of cash to get started. This warning doesn't refer to them. But I've known a number of people (including my cleaning woman) who blew their children's college fund or who took a second mortgage on the house to fill their garage or basement with a multilevel company's product that they were never able to sell. The gimmick is designed to sell everyone possible on buying a lot of product up front.

Most legitimate direct-selling companies make it possible for a person to get into their business for a few hundred dollars or often much less. Again, the DSA will provide a list of companies at your request.

A Chapter 13 Thought

None of us ever has it made; the important thing is that we're making it.

Women in Sales

Sorry fellows, no offense, but women may be superior to you in selling. It's been my observation that the odds are better that a woman will succeed in face-to-face selling than a man of equal talent. Evidence of women's sales success is shown by a recent DSA industry survey, which shows that 82 percent of all direct-sales people are women. For the women reading this book, this is an encouraging reminder that you have some special advantage in this business. If you come to face-to-face selling after having experience as a homemaker, remind yourself of all the excellent preparation you have. For example:

- You are accustomed to having varied responsibilities.

- You've developed an ability to carry a number of projects toward completion at the same time.

- You are especially sensitive to helping customers get what they want because of your prospect-oriented sales approach.

On top of all these advantages you've been operating in a role that traditionally doesn't provide a lot of recognition. In selling, you will find the regular, positive feedback a refreshing benefit.

So, guys, you don't have to be outworked or outperformed, but any feelings of superiority you might have about your sales capabilities versus those of women are unjustified.

Age and Late Bloomers

Some companies have sales management development programs that exclude people over forty years of age. You have to wonder about such a strategy. I've had the good fortune to be associated with a number of incredible people who entered the selling field in their forties, fifties, and even sixties. The highest-producing seller that I ever recruited was fifty-seven when he went into sales after retiring from the clergy. He was among the top twenty sellers in the company's entire sales force of 60,000 people for almost a decade.

Speaking of late bloomers, when I attended the Harvard Advanced Management Program, I had a classmate who was a classic example. Trevor is now one of the six senior officers of the huge Barclay's Bank Organization in Great Britain. But it wasn't easy for him. For many years he held a variety of insignificant positions with the bank. Then something happened. In the next seven years, Trevor earned eleven promotions, a truly remarkable accomplishment.

His meteoric rise during that seven-year period after all those years without promotions is proof that it is rarely too late to get to the top. One of the wonderful things about the human spirit is that individuals can blossom at any stage of their careers *if they decide to take the steps required for success.*

The world is full of people who experienced failures throughout their lives but enjoyed fabulous success in their later years. One of the best known is Colonel Sanders, who started his great restaurant chain at age sixty-five despite major setbacks in his earlier career.

Prep School or Ivy League Background

In many types of business organizations, the particular college or prep school you attended or the social connections you have can have a great impact on whether or not you get that first job. A lot of my attorney friends tell me that the prestige of their law schools was an important factor in their early career successes.

In most face-to-face selling opportunities, your school background and social status don't have a major impact on your upward mobility. The reason is because success in sales depends on your everyday performance. You have to *make* it happen. I've always believed, too, that you can get an outstanding education at most universities in the country if you apply yourself. Conversely, you might manage to earn a degree from an especially prestigious university but not be very well educated.

If you have a strong work ethic, the chances are you've got a leg up in the selling field. I have not seen many big successes in direct selling who came from wealthy families, but I've seen a lot of successful people who have had more than their share of struggles in life.

I hope none of this turns off those lucky ones who were born to wealth.

Weather

One of my major turnoffs is the nightly television weather forecast. It turns me off because there's not a single thing you can do about the weather. I intend to feel good whether it's snowing or raining or whether the sun is shining. Since there's nothing I can do about it, I'm going to have a productive, worthwhile day regardless of what the weather is.

If it's raining, I am reminded that people are likely to be at home. If there's a snowstorm, I am going to call on my neighbor. As a sales manager for direct-sales companies, when we had a snowstorm, I got on the phone and told all my salespeople that "Operation See Your Neighbor" was in effect. They understood that this meant that sales didn't need to stop because of the weather. I have an umbrella and a raincoat in my car, and I'm always ready for the rainy day.

Sweating the Small Stuff

I frequently meet salespeople who are negatively affected by the fact that they have lost an order to someone. It's a dangerous habit; they'll sit around losing five more while stewing over one missed commission or a stolen order. Before they know it, their attitudes have cost them twenty orders. You have to be very careful that you don't get into snits over insignificant matters.

I could give you a whole catalog of examples of this. So if you want to make big things happen, you have to be very careful that you don't sweat the small stuff. This doesn't mean you should never analyze the reasons for a failure. It does mean you should not dwell on any particular failure.

Training

It takes guts to *ask* for training. I made the point earlier that you should not worry about what you don't know. This is true, but it doesn't mean that you don't need training. We all do. There are a variety of ways to get it.

Training can be formal or informal. It can be in the field in front of the prospect, in conversations with your managers on the phone or in person, or it can be in a formal classroom.

Hopefully, you'll join a company that has a good training program. Of course a lot of it is up to you. Do you use the training tools and opportunities that are available to you on an ongoing basis?

Salespeople all too often watch a training video or read a manual when they begin the business, but they overlook the fact that they need to regularly reinforce and renew what they learned in the very beginning. Someone once asked, "How long do you train a salesperson?" The answer was "How long do you want them to be good?" So remember, your training is an ongoing process.

If you get to a point where you assume your training is completed, you may find yourself in a situation like the salesperson who asked his boss why a less-experienced person got a promotion rather than he himself. He said to his boss, "I have ten years experience, and the person you promoted has only three years." The boss replied, "Wrong. You have one year's experience repeated ten times." It's important that you have a learning experience every day, every month, and every year that you are in a position.

Commission Business

Recently, I read an article that said if a company is offering only commissions as compensation and not a salary it should be a "red flag"—a warning not to join that company, because reputable, respectable companies don't give people commission-only opportunities; they pay salaries and commissions.

I personally think this is a lot of baloney. I know a lot of very fine companies that offer incredible opportunities but don't pay salaries. They put it on the line and say, "Look, you'll be paid what you're worth."

I like the commission business because it allows me to earn exactly what I'm worth based on my sales results. When you are paid only on salary remember that your salary is overhead to your company.

When you're on commission, you're a profit-generator for the company. In effect, the income you get is in proportion to the profit your sales generate. How important is this? Very important. It gives you tremendous job security. Organizations that pay people on a commission basis are unlikely to lay people off when the market gets a little soft. And their market probably isn't going to get as soft because their salespeople are going to be out making things happen!

During the major recessions we have had in the years that I have been in direct selling, the companies I've been associated with have had solid sales results. The key salespeople in these organizations sometimes actually increased their personal selling results during recessions. Not that it was easier to sell (I don't believe that it was easier), but I'm sure that everyone worked a little harder to give a good performance.

Several Selling Jobs at the Same Time

With very rare exceptions if you have more than one sales position at a time you are costing yourself money.

Frequently we see examples of professional athletes with multi-million dollar contracts whose athletic performances are negatively affected by "too many briefcases." If an individual is earning megabucks in one profession, it just isn't smart to dabble in other things to the point where he or she kills the goose that laid the golden egg. Most folks can concentrate on only one thing at a time.

Opportunity for Promotion

Salespeople sometimes worry whether there's going to be an opening for them when they are ready for a promotion. It's been my observation in more than twenty-five years in selling that it's rare that there won't be a promotion available for a person who is really ready for it.

If you're interested in upward mobility and are in the selling game, prepare yourself—be a performer—and get the job done. Then when you're ready the odds are very much in your favor that the job will be ready for you.

Prestige of the Selling Profession

Even today a lot of people in this country do not understand the importance and the professionalism of the selling profession. At the risk of offending people in public service or civil service jobs, I've observed that some of these individuals turn up their noses at people who are in face-to-face selling.

The fellow who hired me into direct selling had the right attitude. I asked him about prestige because I was a schoolteacher. I was an educator, as they say down South. He raised his eyebrows and said, "Prestige among whom? The people who count will realize that you have a heck of a lot more prestige when you're making things happen in sales than in your present position." He pointed out that I would be able to influence even more people in a positive way as a successful salesperson than as a teacher.

I've always taken that attitude. But, unfortunately, some people don't understand the selling business and fail to comprehend how vital selling is to free society. They don't know that it wasn't mass production that made America great—it was mass merchandising!

If you are convinced the work you are doing is worthwhile, if you are taking home the big paycheck, and if you are growing personally, that should give you all the prestige you need.

The Car You Drive

Very early in my career, I was happy to be driving a relatively big car. School principals occasionally saw my shiny new car and said, "Gee, you must be making a lot of money on these products you're selling me." My comment was, "We don't make much on each one, but we sell a lot of them."

I doubt if the type of car you drive has any significant impact on the sales you get in most businesses. But remember the point I made earlier in chapter 5, "You Are the Message": The car you drive is *part* of the message. If it's neat and clean and gives you dependable transportation, it makes the statement you need to make.

A former boss of mine summed up my philosophy on the car question. He said some salespeople feel the price of the car they drive will determine their effectiveness in attracting other salespeople. He said that he probably wouldn't want to hire a person who made a career decision on the basis of the kind of car a person drove.

Boredom

This country has a problem today. I saw a statistic that showed that 80 percent of all American workers are bored stiff. The article said that assembly-line workers live for the weekend and consider the other five days in the week to be drudgery.

One of the great benefits of the selling business is this: If you are a person interested in growth, in making things happen, in learning your job, you will never suffer from boredom in face-to-face selling.

Sick Days

"I don't feel good. I need a day off." Familiar words?

I've been blessed with good health. As a matter of fact, I haven't been sick in bed a day in twenty-five years. I have been very fortunate.

It is understandable that someone may occasionally need a sick day for a heavy cold, the flu, or some other malady. But I believe there is a lot of truth to the statement quoted to me by superseller Jan Gilmore, "I don't have time to be sick!"

Yes, I'm skeptical about the individual who claims to be sick every few weeks, taking ten or twelve sick days a year. I've never seen a dynamic leader or a big performer in selling use ten or twelve sick days a year. Feeling good is, to a great extent, a state of mind.

Physical Fitness

So you get in top shape, and it makes you a star in face-to-face selling. That's obviously an over-statement but physical fitness will give you a competitive edge if you want to be a pacesetter. Fitness has a number of benefits. You'll have more of the energy and mental alertness that are so important in this field. If you are in shape, you will undoubtedly have more self-esteem, another vital asset in achieving success.

Equally important, whether we like to admit it or not, prospects react more positively to the salesperson whose appearance indicates that he or she is fit. But to me, personally, the mental outlook I have on days that I've had a brisk thirty to forty-five minutes of exercise is the most important thing. It does all the things for me I just mentioned. I have more energy, I'm more alert, and I feel better about myself.

You need—everyone needs—to have a physical program that suits you, whether it's walking, riding the exercise bike, jogging, swimming, or whatever. Some kind of aerobic exercise may be best. There is definitely a high payoff for the time that you spend keeping physically fit. Some people say, "I just don't have time to have an exercise program." A poor excuse. I personally find that with thirty or forty minutes a day with a good exercise program, I need at least an hour less sleep. So the "time excuse" doesn't stand up. Get in shape. It pays off well.

Changing Jobs or Companies

You have heard the line that a rolling stone gathers no moss. I believe this is generally true; frequent job changes are not wise.

Remember, there's a learning curve in most selling positions. Some individuals give up on selling too quickly. Earlier you learned how the law of averages works. It is important that you don't prejudge what a position can be like when things are not going well. Of course, there are times when making a decision to change companies will be easy. A product line that is not competitive, a company's shaky financial condition, unethical or illegal practices, intolerable management—all are situations that would make it necessary for you to move.

A better type of problem will face you when another company seeks your special talent or skills and makes you an offer you can't refuse. The point I make here is that you should not have "blinders on" just because things are going well for you in your present position. There is a happy medium between always thinking the grass is greener elsewhere and closing your mind to opportunity.

Just be sure that when you consider changing companies, you are doing it for *positive reasons*.

Financial Stability

A rule of thumb: Spend a little less than you make. Salespeople tend to adjust too quickly to increases in their incomes. They make X amount of dollars a week then they double their income for a few weeks. They've been living comfortably on half of the new figure, but immediately adjust to a lifestyle that's twice as expensive, based on commissions they may earn for only a short time.

This can be dangerous. Better to pay yourself a flat salary and put the rest of the money in the bank. Early in my career, I was motivated to achieve financial security by observing that many of the veteran salespeople I was working with didn't have two nickels to rub together. And many had been selling for twenty-five years or more.

What to do? Plan ahead. Example: Take 10 percent out of your earnings each week and put it in a bluechip investment. If you're young, you're bound to be wealthy by the time you're ready to retire.

Handling Success

How do you handle success in face-to-face selling? It's a legitimate concern. Some people get cocky and turn into conspicuous consumers. Even worse some stop doing the very things that made them successful.

This can happen when a salesperson receives a substantial promotion. Moving up the management ladder in a direct-selling organization, I found that it was easier to be the best each time I got promoted because many of the people at my new level had stopped doing the things that enabled them to get the promotion. If they hadn't entirely stopped doing them, they were usually not doing as many of them.

I don't subscribe to the Peter Principle. I don't believe that people usually get promoted to positions they can't handle. I believe people generally are capable of doing the job if they are really committed to doing it. They become incompetent only when they decide they've "arrived" and that work, especially the amount of work that got them there, is no longer necessary.

SUMMARY

In case you are peeking at the back of the book before you've read it, I'll tell you what you'll get out of reading it. Or if you have already read it, I'll remind you of what I've said. *Get as big a slice of life as you can get!* This is not a trial run, this is the real thing! When the opportunity arises, *go for it!* Reach for the stars; you may not reach a star, but you won't come up with a handful of mud, either. *Confront life creatively!* Being the best that you can be means that you need to confront each opportunity you have every day. Creative confrontation means "facing things boldly." It means coming to grips with each of life's challenges rather than hoping that problems will just go away. This means reminding yourself that *everything is a selling job.* (I mean this in a totally wholesome way.) The sales process explained in the book *works.* Use it!

Deliver all that you promise! The growth companies, and the star salespeople of the twenty-first century are going to be those organizations and individuals who are service oriented—those who do a little more for the customer than they have to do. Whoever said, "Help enough others get what they want, and you will get everything you want" was right on the button. ❏

Appendix A

Principles of
Effective Phone Work
and a Sample
Telephone Presentation

TEN BASIC POINTS FOR SUCCESSFUL PHONE WORK

1. Your purpose is usually to introduce yourself or get an appointment—not to sell. The selling will be done at the appointment. (In some cases, you may be selling the prospect on attending a free workshop or seminar.)

2. Sell the prospect on what the appointment or evaluation session will do for him or her. Sell benefits—sell benefits—sell benefits!

3. Convey a sincere, friendly, and helpful attitude on every call, both by your tone and your words. Your mental attitude is the most imporant factor in successful telephoning.

4. Be optimistic. Think success. Show conviction. Be proud of your job and your company.

5. Repeat your prospect's name often.

6. Be tactful in your choice of words, particularly when asking questions.

7. Take the lead in the conversation and keep it. If the prospect takes charge, your chances of getting the prospect to do what you want are greatly reduced.

8. Be alert. Listen to the prospect's reaction to your offer as it progresses. Be ready to capitalize on any sudden or unexpectecl response.

9. Learn to tell when you are wasting your time with a prospect and politely end the conversation.

10. End the conversation once the offer or invitation has been accepted.

After each call, you should not forget to take the following step immediately:

1. Record the results of your call and any follow-up that is required.

TELEPHONE PROSPECTING

Telephone prospecting should be conducted at hours convenient for prospects and appropriate to your business.

"Good evening, Mr./Mrs. _____. My name is _____ and I'm calling for (company). Our company is sponsoring a free seminar on tax-reduction strategies for individuals and families. The seminar will be held at the Marriott O'Hare on June 20 beginning at 7:00 p.m. I would be delighted to mail you a personal invitation if you would like to be our guest."

This is a sample of telephone talk, used by a firm with which I was associated, for the purpose of getting people to attend a free seminar.

Answer to Negative Response

"Mr./Ms._____ , the seminar is purely informative; you will not be asked to purchase anything at this seminar. Our purpose is to introduce our company to you and to show you how the service we perform can help you to assure your own personal financial success. The only investment we ask you to make is that of your time, which you will find to be one of the best investments you will ever make. I would be happy to send you an invitation."

Positive Response

"Fine, I'm sure that you will find this seminar to be highly informative and helpful. Will you be bringing anyone with you? (List number of people.) Thank you. We are looking forward to meeting you at the seminar."

Telephone Confirmation

This confirmation should be used a day or two before the seminar.

"Good evening, Mr./Ms. _____ . My name is _____ from _____ . I'm calling to make sure that you received your invitation to the seminar that our company is sponsoring(time/date/location).

Mr./Ms. _____, I believe you indicated that you would be (bringing a friend with you), (coming alone), (bringing your spouse with you); is that correct? (Confirm.) Mr./Ms. _____, we'll be looking forward to meeting you."

Appendix B

Suggested
Telephone Talk

MAKING A SELLING APPOINTMENT

"Hello, may I please speak to _____? (Wait for a reply.) My name is _____ and (Sue Smith) gave me your name. How are you today?"

At this point it is very important that you wait for a reply. (You will get one.) The goal of this presentation is to keep it as conversational as possible. If you remember this at all times and don't rush, you will get great results! If you can hear that this is a busy time for her, say:

" Can I take a minute, _____, or is this a busy time for you?" (Wait for a reply. If the time is not good, suggest that you will call her later that day, or ask if tomorrow would be better. Be brief! No one wants you to take precious minutes away when she is harried anyway. You then call back at the suggested time.)

If she gives you permission, proceed as follows:

"I was visiting with (Sue) the other day to show her some special materials designed to help prepare her (Bobby) for school, and she thought that you too might like to know what is available. She thought I should give you a call. I would like very much to meet you and explain this (program) to you. Do you have a little time this week that we can talk about it together?" (Wait for a reply. The first thing to do is to suggest a day and time; if that is not convenient, suggest another. You may ask if she wants her husband to see this as well, in order to determine if it is to be an evening appointment.) After you make the appointment, ask if it is necessary to check with her the day before. If she says no, then say you will look forward to meeting her next _____.

There is always the possibility that she will forget the appointment. If she lives far away, or if you want to check the night before rather than take the chance of an unanswered call when you check, don't ask if the appointment is still on! Say instead that you are calling to verify her address:

"Is the number 47 or 49? I couldn't read my handwriting." In other words, assume you still have the appointment and are calling to verify some other information.

If the parent you are calling on has older children, rather than saying that you called on (Sue) to show her material to prepare her children, etc., you can say, "I was visiting with (Sue) the other day to show her about it and thought that you might like some information about it as well. She suggested that I give you a call. I would very much like to . . . ," and proceed to ask for a convenient time for an appointment.

The purpose of a referral call is to *get the appointment*. It is not a good idea to go into a sales presentation on the phone except in response to direct questions. Even under these circumstances, give out only enough to whet the appetite. You want to visit in person so you will have an advantage.

If the prospect seems nervous about committing herself to an appointment, but you feel there is some interest there, suggest mailing information. Generally a review or reprint is a good idea, followed by a call to see if she received it and has any further questions about it.

Remember, each call will bring you closer to a sale. Relax; don't rush it, and above all be flexible in your responses. This is not the only prospect you will get. The next call will bring you wonderfully exciting things—interesting contacts, money, and a host of possibilities. ❏

Index

-A-

-B-

-C-

-D-

-E-

-F-

-G-

-H-

-J-

-L-

-M-

-N-

-O-

-P-

-R-

-S-

-T-

-V-

-W-

Job Search 101:
Getting Started on Your Career Path

Authors: Pat Morton &
   Marcia R. Fox, Ph.D.
ISBN: 1-56370-314-9
Price: $12.95
Pub Date: March 1997

Home But Not Alone
The Parents' Work-at-Home Handbook

Author:
   Katherine Murray
ISBN: 1-57112-080-7
Price: $14.95
Pub Date: May 1997

Beat Stress with Strength
A Survival Guide for Work and Life

Authors:
   Stefanie Spera, Ph.D.
   & Sandra Lanto, Ph.D.
ISBN: 1-57112-078-5
Price: $12.95
Pub Date: March 1997

Jobscape
Career Survival in the New Global Economy

Author: Colin Campbell
ISBN: 1-56370-316-5
Price: $16.95
Pub Date: June 1997

America's Top Military Careers, Revised Edition

Author: U.S. Department
   of Defense
ISBN: 1-56370-310-6
Price: $19.95
Pub Date: March 1997

Healthy, Wealthy, & Wise
A Guide to Retirement Planning

Compiled by the editors
   at Drake Beam Morin
ISBN: 1-57112-081-5
Price: $12.95
Pub Date: July 1997

Inside Secrets of Finding a Teaching Job

Authors: Jack Warner
   and Clyde Bryan
   with Diane Warner
ISBN: 1-57112-079-3
Price: $12.95
Pub Date: April 1997

Be Your Own Business!
A Definitive Guide to Entrepreneurial Success

Edited by Marcia R. Fox, Ph.D.
ISBN: 1-57112-082-3
Price: $16.95
Pub Date: August 1997

Job Savvy, Second Edition
How to Be a Success at Work

Author: LaVerne L.
   Ludden, Ed.D.
ISBN: 1-56370-304-1
Price: $10.95
Pub Date: April 1997

JIST Order Form

Purchase Order #: _____

jist Works, Inc.

8902 Otis Avenue
Indianapolis, IN 46216

Billing Information

Organization Name: _____
Accounting Contact: _____
Street Address: _____
_____
_____
City, State, Zip: _____
Phone Number: ( ) _____

Shipping Information (If Different from Above)

Organization Name: _____
Contact: _____
Street Address: (We *cannot* ship to P.O. boxes)
_____
_____
_____
City, State, Zip: _____
Phone Number: ( ) _____

> **Phone:**
> **1-800-648-JIST**
> **Fax:**
> **1-800-JIST-FAX**
> **World Wide Web**
> **Address:**
> **http://www.jist.com**

Credit Card Purchases:

VISA____ MC____ AMEX____

Card Number: _____
Exp. Date: _____
Name As on Card: _____
Signature: _____

Quantity	Order Code	Product Title	Unit Price	Total

Subtotal	
+5% Sales Tax Indiana Residents	
+Shipping / Handling / Ins. (See left)	
TOTAL	

Shipping / Handling / Insurance Fees

In the continental U.S. add 7% of subtotal:
- Minimum amount charged = $4.00
- Maximum amount charged = $100.00
- FREE shipping and handling on any prepaid orders over $40.00.

Above pricing is for regular ground shipment only. For rush or special delivery, call JIST Customer Service at 1-800-648-JIST for the correct shipping fee.

Outside the continental U.S. call JIST Customer Service at 1-800-648-JIST for an estimate of these fees.

Payment in U.S. funds only!

Please copy this form if you need more lines for your order.

JIST thanks you for your order!